Marriage
can be Great!
...no, really

Guy & Jeannine

with best
wishes for the great years
ahead!

D

La « *Prière quotidienne* » de Saint Thomas d'Aquin:

« Accordez-moi, Dieu miséricordieux, de désirer ardemment ce qui vous plaît, de le rechercher prudemment, de le reconnaître véritablement et de l'accomplir parfaitement, à la louange et à la gloire de votre nom.

Mettez de l'ordre en ma vie, accordez-moi de savoir ce que vous voulez que je fasse, donnez-moi de l'accomplir comme il faut et comme il est utile au salut de mon âme.

Que j'aille vers vous, Seigneur, par un chemin sûr, droit, agréable et menant au terme, qui ne s'égare pas entre les prospérités et les adversités, tellement que je vous rende grâces dans les prospérités, et que je garde la patience dans les adversités, ne me laissant ni exalter par les premières, ni déprimer par les secondes.

Que rien ne me réjouisse ni me m'attriste, hors ce qui me mène à vous ou m'en écarte. Que je ne désire plaire ou ne craigne de déplaire à personne, si ce n'est à vous. Que tout ce qui passe devienne vil à mes yeux à cause de vous, Seigneur, et que tout ce qui vous touche me soit cher, mais vous, mon Dieu, plus que tout le reste.

Que toute joie me dégoûte qui est sans vous, et que je ne désire rien en dehors de vous. Que tout travail, Seigneur, me soit plaisant qui est pour vous, et tout repos ennuyeux qui est sans vous. Donnez-moi souvent de diriger mon cœur vers vous, et, dans mes défaillances, de les peser avec douleur, avec un ferme propos de m'amender.

Rendez-moi, Seigneur Dieu, obéissant sans contradiction, pauvre sans défection, chaste sans corruption, patient sans protestation, humble sans fiction, joyeux sans dissipation, sérieux sans abattement, retenu sans rigidité, actif sans légèreté, animé de votre crainte sans désespoir, véridique sans duplicité, faisant le bien sans présomption, reprenant le prochain sans hauteur, l'édifiant de parole et d'exemple sans simulation.

Donnez-moi, Seigneur Dieu, un cœur vigilant que nulle curieuse pensée ne détourne de vous, un cœur noble que nulle indigne affection n'abaisse, un cœur droit que nulle intention perverse ne dévie, un cœur ferme que nulle épreuve ne brise, un cœur libre que nulle violente affection ne subjugue.

Accordez-moi, Seigneur mon Dieu, une intelligence qui vous connaisse, un empressement qui vous cherche, une sagesse qui vous trouve, une vie qui vous plaise, une persévérance qui vous attende avec confiance, et une confiance qui vous embrasse à la fin.

Accordez-moi d'être affligé de vos peines par la pénitence, d'user en chemin de vos bienfaits par la grâce, de jouir de vos joies surtout dans la patrie par la gloire. Vous qui, étant Dieu, vivez et régnez dans tous les siècles des siècles.

❖

Saint Thomas d'Aquin

Né: ca 1224-25 - dcd: le 7 mars 1274
Fête: le 28 janvier

Marriage
can be Great!
...no, really

Tools & Tips to be
Married for Life
(and Lovin' it!)

Denis Boyd, M.A., R.Psych.

For information, contact:
Denis E. Boyd & Associates Inc.
202 - 1046 Austin Ave., Coquitlam, BC, Canada V3K 3P3
www.denisboyd.com

First Edition

Designed by Avalon Design

ISBN: 978-0-9810827-0-7

For Maureen Elizabeth Boyd, with thanks for all her unity...
happiness is being married to my best friend.

Acknowledgements

Heartfelt gratitude to everyone listed here who played an invaluable role in the evolution of this book.

First of all, I refer to my client "teachers" who have experienced first-hand the trials and tribulations of poor communication but in most cases are able to courageously make the necessary changes to resurrect or revitalize their relationships. They make me look good as a therapist although in reality they are the ones who do all the work!

I thank in particular, several clients who read parts of the manuscript and offered both encouragement and constructive suggestions.

Since I work full days as a psychologist, writing has only been possible on an occasional free weekend. The resulting time span has afforded many opportunities for discussions with friends and colleagues about the focus and content of the material. Rick Hancock, an associate, bet that my book would not see the light of day until 2010; it has been so long since we made the bet that I can't remember what prize I have now won.

Special thanks to Rick and two other associates, Maureen Chapman and Joan Schultz, who graciously read excerpts of the manuscript and offered their input and support. Thank you also to Jennifer Dalla Zanna, Donna Crombie and Farrell Hannah for their valuable suggestions. (Farrell, "Matrimonial Cake: Remember to Include the Dates," would not have worked as a title!)

I respect and admire the compassion and skills of my associate psychologists and counsellors and was delighted that Alivia Maric took the time to read the entire book and offer her insights and affirmations.

Friends and family have also been generous in reviewing parts of the manuscript and have been encouraging and constructive in their feedback. Grateful thanks to Dorothy Casey, Angie Reginato, Trish Legge, Anne Gardiner and Meg and Tom Farr. Extra thanks to Mary Ann Lane for making time to read the entire manuscript and offering her helpful and warm feedback.

Professional writer Jenny Brown and proof-reader Gareth Coghlan have been very helpful in tuning and polishing the book. They assisted in transforming the content into what it is today and have been gentle and straight forward with their advice; I thank them both for their good work. Cailin Green (Avalon Design) has been a godsend, designing our cover and content in a spirit of collaboration and enthusiasm.

Maureen and I have been blessed with tremendous children and daughter-in-law; I wish to thank Joanna, Chris, Carolyn, Geoff and Jolene for their ongoing love, encouragement and creative input.

I also wish to remember my deceased parents, Dwayne and Inger Boyd, who taught me many of my first lessons about marriage.

My wife and very good friend, Maureen, has been instrumental in radically tuning my early cumbersome and convoluted writing efforts. She deserves to be listed as co-author for the endless hours she has spent with me editing the numerous drafts. She has been persistent and yet kindly long-suffering in her attempts to have me say what I need to say in a concise and understandable fashion. More importantly she has shared my unfolding vision for this book and its underlying purpose and has put into practice many of the suggestions outlined here.

Table of Contents

Introduction & Overview

This book has been written for couples who are:

- **Contemplating marriage**
- **In healthy, strong marriages looking for affirmation**
- **In struggling marriages looking for a tune-up**
- **In crisis marriages looking for a complete rebuild**

Background

Most therapists will create a counselling style that is a collection of ideas and suggestions from a variety of schools of thought. When I was studying psychology years ago, one of our professors encouraged each member of our class to develop our own theory or approach to therapy. This book represents my theory of counselling as it relates to marriage, and I call it "Marriage Collaboration Therapy".

The ideas shared in this book originate from encounters with hundreds of couples over the last thirty-two years. My education as a psychologist expanded when I started to counsel, and that education continues to this day.

More than one couple

My clients have been my teachers, and I'm sharing their experiences with you in this book, although their names have been changed to protect the "guilty".

Each couple mentioned in this book is a composite of several couples with similar life experiences. Their stories represent the thousands that have been shared with me over the past three decades. Hopefully you will relate to some of them and benefit from the tools and tips offered. The pronouns "he" and "she" are interchangeable throughout the book.

Denis's Definitions

I find it helpful to use certain terms in my work that catch the essence of a theme, such as "work the middle" which means collaborate, or "bird dogger" for a spouse who has trouble letting an issue go without resolution, or "the Blame Game" for couples who keep focusing on the faults of the other (while often ignoring their own). These definitions I have entitled Denis's Definitions because of the particular spin I have given to the terms or phrases and they are listed in Appendix A.

Marriage Can Be Great! ...no, really

It has been a challenge to find a title that best reflects the intent of this book. I have used the title "Marriage Can Be Great" for my handouts on marriage and for workshops I have conducted for over twenty-five years. I want to offer the assurance that not only can marriage survive, but it can also be a great experience. Because the notion of a great marriage might shock some people, I have added "...no, really" as reassurance.

Healthy marriages make for healthy individuals

"Marriage Can Be Great ...No Really" is a collection of suggestions that have evolved from my interactions with clients who have learned, often the hard way, what it takes to be in a healthy and thriving marriage. We have discovered that although there are sacrifices involved in good intimacy, there is also a wonderful paradox: couples in healthy marriages become healthier as individuals as well.

I suspect most people who marry are not as psychologically strong as they could be. I also believe that these same people become stronger through the life they live as a married couple. Marriage is an education and it matures us.

There are various strategies available to help foster good self-esteem. However, recently I have begun to see a connection between feelings of self-worth and the quality of a person's relationships. I suspect that people who have good connections with other people have healthier self-concepts. In other words, their self-confidence is the product of their healthy intimacy, and not a prerequisite.

What follows is an overview of the book and why I have organized concepts the way I have.

Attitude

"Attitude" is a good place to begin. Some wise soul has stated that "attitude is everything," which may be an over-simplified statement, but there's an element of truth contained in this phrase.

Two attitudes are covered in Chapter 1: first, marriage has to be the top priority in a couple's life, and second, the spouses need to be open to growth. Making the marriage a priority sets the stage for all the other suggestions in the book, which essentially aid in that process. The proposals will only be of value if the reader approaches them with an open mind.

Peace with the Past

The second chapter invites you to review your history and make sure you have no "baggage" that gets in the way of a healthy marriage. These "historical sensitivities" can be strong, but may not surface until a couple is married. They can be overcome or neutralized with the help of your spouse.

Some couples try to circumvent the problems of marriage by living together in a common-law relationship and then decide later, perhaps because of the arrival of a child, to marry each other. Statistics show that these couples have a higher divorce rate than those who didn't live together in the first place. Part of the problem may be that life changes with marriage due to the historical influences that surface.

Unconditional Love

Chapter 3 is about "Unconditional Love" and invites you to love without conditions. Self-love is overrated and misdirected, as one can't fix alone a personal wound created in a relationship. This is why I find marriage work so exciting—the healing that individuals enjoy when they sort out their personal issues within a marriage can be strong and long-lasting. Marriage is where we grow up and heal the wounds of the past.

Talk-Time

One way for a marriage to be a top priority is to spend time together on a daily basis. Chapter 4 is entitled "Daily Talk Time" or "T-Time" for those wishing to be less formal. The four steps of this talk are outlined in detail, along with examples of how to make them real. Usually one spouse struggles with this strategy and may not see the need for such regular conversation. For this person, the T-Time needs to be an experiment conducted with an open mind and heart. Entering the talks with a willingness to hear the other person well (love unconditionally) can make a regular T-Time a valuable strategy for maintaining and enriching the marital bond.

Listening is the key

Listening is the key to healthy intimacy, and for this reason, the longest chapter in the book is entitled "To Listen is to Love" and is preceded by a chapter on "Listening Basics." Most of the chapters in the book mention listening in one way or another and the subject is approached from a variety of angles. When it comes to communication, reactive listening is unfortunately common, and empathic or compassionate listening is an ongoing challenge.

Collaboration

Personality differences are an indication of "balance" and can bode well for mutual growth. There needs to be a willingness to work with the differences in hopes of creating collaborative decisions. The seventh chapter discusses typical differences between spouses and gives examples of how to work with the strengths and weaknesses of each couple. The collaboration process strengthens the couple while often leading to excellent decision making.

Time-Out/Time-In

To keep things safe while talking over the day or trying to collaborate, there is a Time-Out/In technique outlined in Chapter 8. One spouse is usually not very comfortable in arguing about issues. This person may avoid topics or bail out early if he thinks things could get tense. The Time-Out/In approach is a safety valve which, if agreed on beforehand, can give a couple a break in the action, and an opportunity to calm down. They can then move on to self-analysis and self-correction.

Forgiveness

Forgiveness is not dealt with extensively in psychological literature, which is a shame, as it is a very important step for moving beyond disappointment and upset.

Conflict is unavoidable in a healthy relationship where both spouses share their differing perspectives, or even in routine discussion undermined by fatigue or distress. Forgiveness allows each person to move beyond their grudges so as to "start again" many times over in their journey as a couple.

The Rebuild

Some crises (an affair, for example) are very challenging for couples to overcome, even with forgiveness. These issues are explored in the tenth chapter, which is entitled "After the Crisis – The Rebuild." Spouses rebuilding their relationships after a near ending will pass through challenges unique to their situation. Trust has been violated or damaged and it takes time to regenerate. A couple may be doing well in this process of re-connection, but not realize it due to some of the issues that arise.

Laugh, Play and Encourage

The book ends on a positive note with "Laugh, Play and Encourage." Many spouses are so busy raising children and making a living that they forget to make time to have fun. Shared humour is enjoyable, as is playing in ways that satisfy both members of the marriage. Learning to love another person "the way he wants to be loved" is part of the education that marriage offers to its participants.

Feel free to use this book as a manual or reference to be revisited many times in the future. The suggestions are often simple in theory, and yet difficult to put into practice.

Let me suggest that you read the book from beginning to end the first time, and then use it as a reference thereafter. The ideas in the book are presented in sequence and build upon one another.

So, you now have a little background and an overview. Read on with my best wishes for a great marriage!

Let's Get Started

Meet the Teachers -
12 Couples whose challenges might sound familiar

A few months into my practice, I started to realize that my clients were becoming some of my greatest teachers. They didn't understand jargon or sophisticated psychological theories. They were just immersed in real life and the struggles associated with trying to be intimate. They needed to be heard, but they also wanted help and practical ideas. I soon learned that the most helpful psychology was sharing the down-to-earth experiences of other couples in similar situations.

You will now meet twelve couples whose names are fictitious, but whose issues will sound familiar. They are introduced simply as a way to showcase the stories that will hopefully be of value to you as you attempt to improve your marriage or other friendships.

Sometimes the same point is made more than once with different scenarios. Presenting an idea from different perspectives helps teach the lesson to a wider audience. Although the names have been changed, these stories are based on real life experiences.

Here's how these examples will be laid out:

1. The first part of each story represents an issue or challenge, which will later be explained in the **What is Happening Here?** section.

2. Next, you will find the **TEAM TOOLS** box, which offers suggestions for change. I have used the term **TEAM TOOLS** to emphasize that a couple is a team and both spouses have a responsibility to make necessary changes in attitude or behaviour. Team members help each other when the going gets rough so that the team (i.e. the marriage) benefits.

3. Following **TEAM TOOLS** is the final part of each section that shows, in most cases, an alternative outcome to the original scenario.

4. After some of the stories, you will find a section called **Your Turn** which allows you to write your own revision of the original story. Cover the final section with a piece of paper and then on a note pad, write your own suggestion for an improved scenario based on the suggestions offered in **TEAM TOOLS**.

5. At the end of each segment you will find a **TIP** that will act as a summary statement. All tips are listed in Appendix B.

CHAPTER ONE

Attitude

What is your attitude towards marriage?

• It is not possible for people to change.	Y	N
• I am the way I am and should not have to change to suit anyone, including my spouse.	Y	N
• It is not right to expect or ask another person to change an aspect of who they are or how they handle situations.	Y	N
• Work is my number one priority.	Y	N
• My children are my number one priority.	Y	N
• I worry about getting too close to my spouse.	Y	N
• I worry about being controlled or badly hurt in my relationship.	Y	N
• My spouse and I are very different people and are increasingly so with the passage of time.	Y	N

Attitude is everything!

How did you fare in the above quiz? If you answered "Yes" to two or more of the above questions, you may want to read on to find out how to tune up and strengthen your marital relationship. Even if you answered "No" to all the questions, please don't close the book! There may be a few nuggets of information that you can pass on to friends or family.

A change in attitude is the first step towards enriching your marriage, and the following examples of "real life" couples will demonstrate why this is so important. But let's start at the beginning with the most crucial point to remember:

Your marriage is your most important relationship!

In order for a marriage relationship to reach its full potential, it needs to be at the top of a couple's priority list. Not second. Not penciled in on the 'B' list. No, it needs to be number one! (In single parent families, the children are number one. When a parent re-marries, the children share the number one spot with the new spouse.)

It's very easy to take a relationship for granted. However, this may often lead to a neglect of the other person's feelings and the likelihood of disrespectful familiarity. One example could be expecting your spouse to always do certain chores or behave in predictable ways.

When children arrive, they tend to take over our lives. When our first child was born, I immediately called my parents to share our wonderful news with them. My mother asked me whether it was a boy or a girl, and I asked her to tell me. She guessed it was a girl, I said "Yes," and we both cried. It was a poignant moment that signalled a major change in both of our lives. My mother had entered a new stage of her life as a grandmother (Nana), and was thrilled to do so. Maureen and I had become new parents, and as a consequence, our marriage entered a new phase.

Children bring out the best in us as well as the worst. For me, it was a period of discovery about new facets of my personality I didn't know existed. For example. I never knew I could speak so loudly until I became a father! On the other hand, having children also revealed a warm and tender side of me that I hadn't been aware of until then.

Being a parent can be a wonderful and deeply meaningful experience, but it can also be a demanding and exhausting one. Our children can easily become the main focus of our lives, and as a result, it becomes nearly impossible to find time alone as a couple. On top of this new stress, work commitments outside of the family can absorb the time and energy of one or both partners. Therefore, the big challenge is to keep the marital bond as your main priority in spite of the other demands vying for your time each day.

I once asked a group of parents of pre-schoolers who the most important person(s) was in their lives. Most of the parents responded, predictably, that their children were. Wrong answer! The relationship with your spouse has to be number one. A mother in the group disagreed, saying that she had heard a radio personality (apparently an expert on family relationships) state that the child has to be the first priority. Even if you identify with this viewpoint and insist on making your child number one, you need to pretend that "Dad" or "Mom" is first. Why? Because children love their parents equally, and if they sense that they are being favoured over the other parent, they will feel guilty.

You also need to be "open to growth."

When I speak to engaged couples, I always ask them if they are open to growth. If they aren't, I suggest they avoid getting married because marriage will challenge them to change. Specifically, each spouse will ask the other to make some changes in their attitude or behaviour. Some people (see Frank and Felicity below) are happy the way they are and don't plan to change in any way. Such people should perhaps remain single because a healthy marriage requires that each spouse be open to making some requested changes.

Here's a concept you may never have considered: not only does marriage change us, but it also provides us with the opportunity to finally grow up! In fact, the marriage relationship takes on the same power and significance of our birth family, and because of this, there is power in the marital bond. Within the marriage relationship we have the unique opportunity to grow beyond our past, and to some degree, to recreate ourselves.

Interestingly, those aspects of our lives that a spouse asks us to change are often the very aspects of our lives that most need changing. Even if we lived in a community setting our companions would ask us to make the same changes.

If a couple doesn't make their marriage a priority and fails to have an attitude of openness to growth and change, power struggles can ensue. The relationship can also become neglected or lost in the busyness of everyday life, and requests for change will invariably lead to arguments, polarization or distancing.

If there is openness to growth, the process of change can be less difficult. At times you will feel discomfort and even some pain, as receiving feedback can be like a "pruning" experience. But such pruning leads to new growth, and changes are usually met with appreciation by everyone involved. When we allow ourselves to grow, we have to remember that changes take time to unfold, so we shouldn't become discouraged.

BETH AND BOB

Introduction: Beth and Bob are newlyweds. Like most couples, they have their similarities and their differences. Bob is a self-confessed "neat freak" and Beth is more laid back. They are adjusting to each other.

I Have to Accept Her the Way She Is

Bob loves Beth and hopes to raise a family with her; however, he finds her to be messy at times, and this bothers him. She becomes absorbed in her hobbies and doesn't share their common household duties. Bob realizes that Beth works part-time and wants to make the most of her spare time, but this situation still concerns him.

Bob wants to talk with Beth about the job sharing, but he's reluctant to do so, as he believes that he has to accept Beth for who she is.

WHAT *is happening here?*

Bob is correct in thinking that he has no right to demand that Beth change in any way. However, as her husband and partner for life, he has every right to ask her to change certain ways of thinking or acting. Whether she does so or not is up to her. Beth also has the right, as the marital partner of Bob, to ask him to change as well.

TEAM TOOLS

Trying to force change upon a spouse is unwise. Marriage partners are different in many ways, but one of their similarities is their strength of character. Telling each other what to do can lead to power struggles and mutual frustration. Asking the spouse to *consider* some changes, however, is acceptable and, at times, necessary.

A change in attitude:

Bob invites Beth to have a cup of tea and they begin to discuss their day. He asks her if he can bring up an issue that bothers him, and Beth encourages him to do so. He talks about the clutter in the home and his wish that it could be cleaned up. Beth is surprised that this matter bothers him, as he hadn't mentioned it before. She says that she tunes out the clutter, as she enjoys her hobbies. She asks Bob if he's still willing to do some cleaning-up as well, and he agrees to continue to do his part. Beth says that she'd like it if Bob would make more time to landscape the yard and he says he will make this a priority.

TIP: It is OK to ask your spouse to change.

FRANK AND FELICITY

Introduction: Frank and Felicity have been married for eleven years and have two children. Frank works hard and believes that his family is his first priority, and his primary contribution is his role as breadwinner. He enjoys time with his friends and admits he's not a big "family man." His father also worked long hours and had little time for his children, and this is the model Frank had as a child.

Felicity has a need to feel secure, and was initially comforted by Frank's dependability as a provider. Now, with the children on the scene, she wants more family time. In particular, she wants her husband to do more with their kids on his own and be a more involved father. Felicity also wants a closer relationship with her husband.

Frank gets his "relationship needs" met with his friends and thinks Felicity should do the same with hers. Before this couple married, Frank was up front about his commitment to sports and friends, and

Felicity didn't take him seriously. She thought she could convince him to change over time.

I'm the Same Guy She Married

Felicity is frustrated and lonely. Although they each participate in a number of activities with their children, Frank is seldom home, and therefore, most of the family duties fall upon Felicity. Frank has reluctantly agreed to come for counselling to talk about "his wife's problems."

According to Frank, family is first on his priority list. He firmly states that he works demanding hours only to maintain a certain standard of living. He thinks that providing financial stability is his way of showing his commitment to his wife and children. However, because he works these long hours, he says that he needs time with his buddies to unwind.

WHAT is happening here?

In spite of his justifications, Frank is making his job the number one priority. His number two priority is his own relaxation and recreation. His family, therefore, comes in a distant third. Although Frank is very aware of what he likes and dislikes, he has little idea of what is important to his wife and children.

When Felicity raises the issue of wanting a relationship with her husband and for him to spend more time with their children, he becomes annoyed and tells Felicity to stop trying to change him. He says that she knew what he was like when they married, and he hasn't changed since then. To Felicity, he doesn't appear to want to change.

TEAM TOOLS

Some people enjoy being single and carry that mindset into their relationship. **Marriage is a "team lifestyle" and in order to be successful, the relationship needs to become a top priority!** One fellow put it well when he said that when he and his wife married, there was now an "us" which needed to be cared for, as opposed to just a "me."

> When two people marry, they are no longer single and they need to plan their lives and priorities accordingly. This doesn't mean that a spouse no longer has a personal life; rather, he plans his activities in consultation with his wife, since whatever he does now impacts her life as well. She does the same thing, so that her personal pastimes don't erode the marriage.
>
> **When a husband or wife is living as a married single, there's a risk that the relationship will deteriorate and be lost!**

The story continues:

Frank is now coming home from work earlier to make more time for Felicity and the tensions around this topic are easing. However, he still plays hockey three times a week and arrives home late after drinks at the rink.

Felicity continues to talk with Frank about cutting back on his sports and other activities with the boys, but Frank is not impressed, as he has already reduced his work hours. It seems to him that there's "no pleasing" Felicity.

WHAT is happening here?

Frank was up front with Felicity before they married about his sports activities being a big part of his life. The time for Felicity to challenge Frank would have been before their marriage and not afterwards.

Perhaps if Frank had realized that Felicity wouldn't have married him under such circumstances, he may have examined his priorities more closely and promised to make adjustments. Felicity's current need to have time with her husband is appropriate, and his time-consuming commitment to sports is not.

TEAM TOOLS

Token changes aren't enough to reassure your spouse that you are considering her needs when making decisions. The underlying attitude must also change if one's behaviour conflicts with the needs of the other. Frank isn't open to the changes needed to move from the single to the married life.

The story ends:

Felicity decides that she won't continue living with a husband who isn't committed to her and the children. She initiates a separation, and learns soon afterwards that Frank has also been having an affair.

TIP: Be honest about expectations from the get-go.

GORD AND GINA

Introduction: Gord and Gina have been married for about five years. Gina is a self-contained person who thinks things through thoroughly, but shares little of the process. Her husband, Gord, is the opposite in that he thinks out loud in a stream-of-consciousness manner. During their dating, Gina was fairly forthcoming with Gord, and Gord was careful not to overwhelm her with his openness. They got along well. Once they were married, however, there was a shift in their behaviours. It was as if the extra efforts made during dating were no longer necessary now that they were in a committed relationship.

Change Comes With the Territory

Gina likes her husband's openness. This trait was attractive to her when they first met. Gord, in turn, was attracted to Gina's shy personality.

Over time though, Gord has become frustrated at Gina's reluctance to share her thoughts candidly. In turn, she is bothered by him talking so much in general.

WHAT is happening here?

Gord and Gina are a good match. They balance each other with their different communication styles. The novelty, however, has worn down, and both of them would like to see some change in each other. This isn't unusual in a marriage.

TEAM TOOLS

When couples date, they often try hard to impress each other ✗ by appearing to be similar. Once they enter into marriage, there is often not the same effort to please as there had been during the courtship or dating period. It can be a shock for both spouses to realize that their husband or wife is not a mirror image of themselves.

It has been said that couples divorce resenting the qualities they used to love in each other. Rather than adjust in an attempt to meet each other's needs, many couples will power ⁷ struggle, losing their marriage in the process.

Personality differences between spouses should be celebrated as they are an indication of a good match. There is potential for each person to learn from the other. The differences also make things interesting, as each spouse is presented with new ways of interacting with life. Identical personalities might become bored with each other or clash continuously. Spouses need to adjust to and for one another.

A change in attitude:

After some coaching, Gord and Gina now have reasonable expectations of each other. Gina is starting to share her thoughts and ideas with Gord in normal conversation and this pleases him. It's good for Gina to learn how to do this, as she is now more relaxed and surprised at how much more quickly some issues are resolved by talking them out.

It makes Gina happy that Gord is cutting back on his endless chattering. For her part, she's responding more to his feelings. Gord is trying to hold back and offer opportunities for Gina to respond.

TIP: Adjust to one another and for one another.

He Has to Change Because He Wants To

Gina is bothered by the messy garage. She wants to ask Gord to do some things differently, but she doesn't want him to alter his behaviour just for her. She would rather he change because he wants to. She suspects that he's okay with his priorities, as he seems comfortable with a messy garage. She's now thinking that maybe she should just put up with the mess.

WHAT is *happening here?*

Gina is holding back, as she doesn't think her concerns are reason enough for Gord to consider a change. She doesn't want to ask him to make changes and then have him resent her later.

TEAM TOOLS

In healthy marriages, each spouse changes some of their behaviours out of love for the other. However, it's important that the change be embraced with sincerity and not be made begrudgingly.

By keeping her concerns internal, Gina doesn't allow Gord to tell her how he feels about what bothers her. She has a right as a spouse to ask him to take a look at an issue. *Asking* for something is different than demanding it. Gina can ask Gord to change, and if he changes because of her asking, that is motive enough.

Some wives or husbands think that their spouse "should just know what they want" and do it without being coached. They think that if the other person is asked to do something differently, he won't do it sincerely. It's as if being asked means that the husband isn't changing because he wants to. I often ask spouses if their mates always do what they suggest, and the answer is "No." My point is that a spouse will only change if he wants to, regardless of who asks him.

Even though Gord may feel no need to make a change, he may be willing to do things differently because of Gina's concerns. By doing so, he shows his love for her in a practical way.

A change in attitude:

Gina decides to tell Gord how she feels, and is not surprised that he doesn't think his mess is a big deal. He does, however, acknowledge Gina's irritation, and agrees to make some time to sort through the mess. He asks Gina if she would be willing to help and she agrees to.

TIP: Don't expect your spouse to be a mind reader.

Growth Comes With the Territory

When Gina and Gord attend a party, Gina feels more comfortable waiting for people to reach out to her, whereas Gord chats easily with a variety of people, many of whom he hasn't met before. Gord often pushes Gina to come out of her shell, and the more he does this, the more reserved she becomes. She has even opted out of some gatherings because of her discomfort, and Gord has either stayed home or gone alone. He ends up feeling resentful.

Although Gina admires Gord's sociable nature, she's annoyed by the way he talks to everyone in the room at a social event and ignores her. She's beginning to resent his outgoing personality.

WHAT is happening here?

This couple have typical differences in their personalities: one is outgoing and the other is reserved. They see the value in socializing as a couple, but their differences have become a problem. Rather than learn from each other and approach social gatherings in a collaborative fashion, they are each doing what's comfortable to them.

TEAM TOOLS

Marriage is an education. It's important to be open to the coaching of a spouse. Through encouragement and by example, the strengths and needs of one spouse call forth the potential of the other.

A change in attitude:

Gord and Gina decide to celebrate their differences. They realize that they can learn from each other and accept feedback. At Gord's encouragement, Gina has been taking some risks and starting conversations with other people, rather than waiting for them to come to her. She's slowly building her confidence. She will likely never be as outgoing as her husband, but she is more so now than she was in the past.

For his part, Gord is learning to keep in touch with Gina when at an event. He is still very outgoing, but he now makes it a priority to keep in touch through eye contact and conversation with his spouse.

TIP: Marriage calls forth our potential.

HANNA AND HARVEY

Introduction: Hanna and Harvey have been married for over twenty years. Like Gord, Hanna is more outgoing, and like Gina, Harvey is more reserved. Hanna and Harvey have improved in many ways because of their collaborations as a couple. Harvey is not messy per se, but he isn't as "house conscious" as Hanna.

More Growth

Harvey and Hanna are out for a walk with their dog and are talking about their day. They pass by a little house with an ambulance parked out front. Harvey tells Hanna that he knows who lives there, and that the fellow has a heart condition.

Hanna suggests that he go into the house to see if he can be of support. Harvey, who is shy, balks at the idea and says that he would just be in the way. Hanna urges Harvey to go into the house, and he becomes frustrated. He says that it's not a good idea, and they continue on their walk in silence.

WHAT is happening here?

When urged by Hanna to go into the house of his friend, Harvey rebels at the idea. He uses the excuse that he will be in the way, but the real reason is that he's uncomfortable with it. Even when Hanna asks him a second time, he says "No," and feels frustrated with her for pushing him. Their dialogue has been interrupted, and they go on in silence. Hanna is probably also frustrated, as she thinks her idea is good, and doesn't understand why Harvey wouldn't want to help a friend, as she would have done.

TEAM TOOLS

Personal growth is a lifelong task for most of us. Many people attend individual counselling sessions with the hope of overcoming their depression, anxiety, or low self confidence. However, many personal problems originate from dysfunctional early life relationships. Doesn't it make sense that the solution to the problem or challenge lies within a relationship?

If a malfunctioning relationship created the wound, it makes sense that a functioning relationship can be a part of the repair process. Spouses are in an enviable position to help each other with personal growth challenges.

When spouses are open to learning from each other, there is a tendency to take each other's suggestions seriously, even if they cause discomfort.

Harvey and Hanna's incident above could have had a very different outcome if Harvey had been open to and respectful of Hanna's input. If Harvey remembers that he is growing emotionally and that Hanna's suggestions can often be useful (if somewhat challenging), he will have the courage to move out of his comfort zone.

Here is another way the above story could have unfolded:

Hanna urges Harvey to go into the house. Although Harvey is uncomfortable with the idea, he knows that many of Hanna's suggestions are worth considering. Her ideas challenge him, and when he follows through, he usually experiences good results.

Harvey tentatively approaches the open front door of the house. The ambulance crew is sitting at the kitchen table with the wife of Harvey's friend. When she sees Harvey, she gets up and immediately comes towards him and gives him a hug. She introduces him to the ambulance crew. She tells him that her husband is in his room and that he should say hello. Harvey's friend is sitting on his bed in his pyjamas shaking like a leaf, in the midst of an anxiety attack. Harvey is able to sit with him for a time and help him to calm down.

TIP: **Your spouse can help you grow in confidence.**

The Closet Doors

Hanna and Harvey have a closet in the entrance area of their home. Hanna asks everyone in the family to keep the doors closed, as it looks better that way. Harvey doesn't notice or care whether the doors are open or closed. However, this issue keeps resurfacing, as it bothers Hanna. It also frustrates her that Harvey doesn't take her request seriously.

WHAT is happening here?

Hanna has a preference for closed closet doors and makes it known to her family. Kids will be kids and tend to ignore such information, and Harvey doesn't see the importance of the request; for him, it's no big deal. Hanna feels helpless, as she wants to create a harmonious environment for visitors.

TEAM TOOLS

Each spouse has preferences that differ from those of the other. There's a very human tendency to only value one's own ideas and to reject those of the other person. However, to embrace the preferences of our spouse can be a means of demonstrating love.

Harvey realizes that he and Hanna have different priorities and he also realizes that at the top of his priority list is Hanna. Because she is important to him, he's able to make some of her preferences important to him as well.

Your Turn ...

(Cover the section below and write on a note pad how you might re-solve this issue.)

Harvey doesn't like to see Hanna frustrated and he decides to take her request seriously. He makes closing the closet doors his priority as well, and tells their four children to do the same, and to pick up their shoes while they're at it. Because both mother and father are on the same page, the kids begin to respect the request, and Hanna feels happier now that she is being supported.

TIP: Love by honouring the preferences of your spouse.

JOHN AND JOAN

Introduction: John and Joan have been dating for a number of months and are doing well. They have both been married before, and Joan has three children who are now in their early teens. John gets along well with them. Joan wants a deeper commitment because although they enjoy each other's company, there's little substance to their relation-ship. Both Joan and John are somewhat "commitment phobic," but Joan is interested in facing her fears and moving ahead.

Co-Dependent

Joan and John have discussed the possibility of marriage. Joan is noticing, however, that when she asks John about his feelings on certain topics, he backs off. She's at the point where she's worried about the lack of personal output from John, so she raises this issue with him. He says that they will talk next week.

Next week arrives and he delays until the weekend. Eventually it occurs to Joan that John isn't going to open up with her. She tells him that they need to get more personal, or they will break up. John opts to break up and Joan is shocked and hurt.

WHAT *is happening here?*

This couple enjoy each other's company, but Joan is interested in something deeper, particularly with the possibility of marriage on the horizon. Joan has noticed that John doesn't share many of his feelings, particularly about his goals and dreams, and she wonders who he really is.

They each find it hard to be on their own, and John, in particular, likes to keep busy and have friends around him all the time. He doesn't have the same need for deep personal conversation that Joan does, and it annoys him that she brings it up all the time. He wonders why she can't just let it alone and have fun.

TEAM TOOLS

Many people grow up with attachment issues. They may not have had their emotional needs well met earlier in life, but they survived as best they could. John and Joan have had some losses in their histories that haven't been well debriefed or grieved.

John is afraid to open up with Joan, as he knows deep inside that it will lead to more commitment. If this happens, he will be vulnerable and could be hurt again. John had experienced this when his father left his mother when John was eleven.

John is dependent upon Joan for companionship, but little more. Joan is somewhat dependent, but she also has a sense that something more is needed and pushes for it. This may make her slightly less dependent than John.

Having fun and spending time together can naturally lead to an interest in a deeper commitment. People who are afraid of commitment have trouble "opening up" because they have fears of being controlled or hurt. In order to stay safe, the couple attempts to keep things light. When one partner presses for more commitment, the other person may at first appear to cooperate with the plan.

The story continues:

John and Joan haven't seen each other for about two months and Joan is beginning to get on with her life. Then John calls her and asks to meet. He tells her that he misses her and that he will commit and share more of himself. Joan is excited and pleased.

After a week or two of socializing with no meaningful conversation, Joan begins to pressure John for more personal sharing. He tells her that he's open to it, but not just yet. He continues to delay. Joan becomes frustrated and applies some pressure and John surprises her by angrily telling her that she's harassing him. He then withdraws.

It looks to Joan like John has had second thoughts and has left the relationship. She is hurt and tempted to lower her standards so that John will be with her. Joan also doesn't like to be on her own. When Joan points out to John his delaying tactics, he becomes angry. He tells her that he can't handle her demands, and then he leaves.

WHAT is happening here?

Because John doesn't like to be alone, he has returned to Joan with promises to give more of himself in the relationship. He has appeased her for the moment. However, when she reminds him of his promise, he delays as long as possible, and may secretly hope that Joan will back down. She is tempted to but doesn't, and so he withdraws. He wants to be around her, but not at the expense of his independence. He has a fear that if he gets closer to Joan he will be unable to "have a life."

TEAM TOOLS

Some people need to always have someone around, but they don't feel comfortable going into depth in a relationship. Conversely, others who can be on their own are able to make a commitment to share their lives together.

If one partner becomes unhappy with the "on again/off again" contact, she will pressure further for something more. The other option is to end the relationship. It often turns out that a person who is afraid to commit won't commit to either stay or go. The reluctance to commit one way or another can leave a couple living in "limbo."

The story continues:

Joan is disappointed that John is promising one thing, but is delivering another. She's tempted to back down when he gets angry with her. She wonders if she's wanting too much from him, and shares her doubts with a friend. The friend tells Joan that her expectations are very reasonable. In spite of this feedback, Joan doesn't end the relationship.

Not long after withdrawing in anger, John calls Joan and he is upset. He misses her and wants to get back together. He promises that he'll open up and be more committed. Can he come over right away? Joan is moved by his tears and says that he can come over and they have a warm reunion.

After a few days of "business as usual," Joan tells John that she wants to talk with him. He delays, becomes annoyed with her, and then withdraws, only to call back a few days later, in tears. Joan, once again, allows John to come over and the cycle repeats yet again.

WHAT is happening here?

Although Joan seeks advice after doubting her expectations, she continues to be open to John's promises. To her credit, she does eventually call him to task, but this leads to yet another crisis.

John finds it hard to be on his own and he panics. He wants the company of a relationship, but is unwilling to enter it emotionally. It's as if the boy of eleven has returned and is expressing his fears of being left alone. John, however, is not eleven (at least physically) any longer, and he can realistically take care of himself. Joan reinforces John's insecurity when she feels sorry for him and lets him come back.

TEAM TOOLS

The level of commitment in a relationship needs to meet the needs of both partners. It's important for John and Joan to break the "on again/off again" cycle. Joan can listen to John's fears and convey her understanding of his upset, and yet stick to her plan. She can encourage John to spend some time on his own and to have short periodic visits with her where they slowly deepen their intimacy. It is advisable for him to learn to be satisfied with his own company, and then to evaluate whether he is willing to commit.

A change in attitude:

Joan hasn't heard from John for a few days, but knows that it's only a matter of time before he calls. He does, and asks to come over for a visit. Joan tells him that it would be better if they didn't see each other for a time. John sounds desperate on the phone and begins to cry. Joan acknowledges his upset and fear, but encourages him to spend some time on his own. John hangs up in anger.

A few days later, he calls again and asks Joan for coffee. They meet and chat about superficial things. Joan asks John if he has thought about her suggestion and he says that he has. He admits to being fearful of being on his own, and at the same time, equally fearful of getting close to Joan. He'd like to see her occasionally, and to learn to open up slowly. He knows it will be good for him to spend time on his own, but it scares him. He admits to feeling less fearful having talked about it a little with Joan.

TIP: Standing firm can help others confront issues from the past.

OSSIE AND OLIVIA

Introduction: Ossie and Olivia have tried hard to remain strong individuals over their years of marriage, and enjoy different interests and activities. They grew up at a time when couples tended to spend a lot of time together whether they wanted to or not. They are determined not to follow the same path. The result of this sort of "independence" in their relationship is that they rarely see each other.

My Taste Is Different

Ossie likes country music and Olivia likes classical. She has a subscription to a series of concerts, and attends with a friend who shares her taste in music. When a big name country act comes to town, Ossie attends the concert with a friend.

Because they are busy with their jobs and family activities, Ossie and Olivia find it hard to get together for a date. When one offers a date option, the other isn't interested.

WHAT is *happening here?*

Ossie and Olivia are aware that they need to spend more time together, and both become frustrated with the other's lack of availability. They realize that their musical preferences are contributing to the problem. However, they are missing the point. Interest in music needs to be secondary to their interest in each other.

TEAM TOOLS

When a couple have a chance to do something together, it's irrelevant which activity they choose. In fact, because of different interests, it may be impossible to find a shared activity. The main goal is to spend time together and make the relationship the focus, even if the activity isn't the first choice of one of the spouses. Who knows, Ossie may become an opera nut and Olivia may end up learning to line dance.

Your Turn ...

(Cover the section below and write on a note pad how you might resolve this issue.)

Ossie offers to go to a symphony concert with Olivia because by doing so, he is spending time with her. Olivia, in turn, offers to go to a country concert because this will allow her to spend time with Ossie. This couple realize that their marriage is their number one priority, and they are less concerned about how they spend time with each other. Making small sacrifices like these helps this couple appreciate each other more.

TIP: **The relationship counts, not the activity.**

Your Plan Is My Plan

Olivia and a business colleague, Peg, go on a business trip to another part of the province, which involves being on the road for three or four days. While driving, Peg points out various birds she notices. Olivia has never had much interest in birds, but becomes more curious as Peg points out various species to her.

After Olivia returns home, she starts thinking that she would like to head out to a wildlife refuge and see what birds are passing through. She's uneasy about mentioning this idea to Ossie, as she doesn't want him to think she's odd by wanting to go "bird watching" of all things.

Olivia musters her courage and tells him her idea. She asks if he would like to accompany her to the refuge. Without batting an eye, Ossie says yes. Olivia is delighted.

WHAT is happening here?

Olivia is developing a new interest, which she knows will not likely be a priority for Ossie. Yet because he is a priority to her, she wants to share the idea with him, and therefore, asks him if he wants to tag along.

TEAM TOOLS

When a spouse is open to his partner's interests and appreciates the time he spends with her, the bond between them is enhanced. As mentioned earlier, the interests of one spouse can be embraced by the other as a way of affirming the relationship.

Attitude is everything:

Olivia is surprised by Ossie's response to her request. When she tells him this, he simply says that if this is a new interest for her, then that's good enough for him. He wants to hang out with her and it doesn't matter much what they do.

The interesting outcome is that not only does Ossie go along with Olivia to the refuge, but he gets into it and starts to develop an interest in birds as well!

TIP: Stretch into the world of the other and enhance intimacy.

TINA AND TOM

Introduction: Tina and Tom have been married for seven years and have just had their third child. They both work full time and share the home chores. They adore their children and try to spend time with them whenever possible. If asked the question "Who is your number one priority?" they would answer "Our kids."

Family Life

Tom and Tina's baby is not sleeping through the night and their three-year-old is a bundle of energy. After spending each day at work and each evening caring for their children, they fall into bed exhausted, having not found any moment to be alone with each other. They both have a sense that they are drifting apart, but there seems to be no time to do anything about it!

WHAT is happening here?

Like so many new parents, Tom and Tina are very busy indeed. Their number one priority has become their three delightful and demanding children. There is no time being spent on the marriage: no time for a date night, and more importantly, no time each day for a little one-on-one conversation with each other.

TEAM TOOLS

Any relationship will suffer if it is taken for granted and ignored; the marriage relationship is no exception. Sometimes a couple will use busyness as an excuse to not spend time together, but in reality, they may be afraid of a disagreement or conflict. With practise, a couple can learn to open up safely.

If Tom and Tina make time together a priority and find a few moments each day to talk with each other, they will be pleased with the results.

A change in attitude:

Tom and Tina know that their marriage won't survive on "autopilot." They manage to find a small window of opportunity for some conversation just after their kids go to bed, and are able to tune into each other's moods in a constructive fashion. In spite of their hectic lives, they believe they have a good connection, and have noticed that they don't squabble with each other like many of their friends do on a regular basis.

TIP: **Finding time alone strengthens the bond.**

Playing With the Kids vs. Cleaning Up

Because Tina works full time, she loves to play with her children when she gets home from work. The house is usually cluttered, which bothers her, but time spent playing is more important to her and the children.

Tom likes to come home to a neat house. He's tired and finds the chaos in the home distressing. He has suggested that Tina clean up if she is the first to arrive home, like he does himself.

Tina tells him that cleaning up is "not a priority for her" and that she thinks it's more important to spend quality time with the children. Tom thinks the tidying should be done first and the children can have their time later. He wants their eldest child to help with cleaning up as well.

WHAT is *happening here?*

Tina and Tom have been stuck on this issue for some time, as they are locked into their own priorities. They find themselves bogged down in a power struggle.

TEAM TOOLS

Knowing the importance of collaboration doesn't always make it easier to achieve. Spouses can try discussing their preferences and then work towards a joint solution that they can both live with. This discussion may even happen during a few different conversations. The exciting thing is that the result is an affirmation of their love for each other. (For more information about consultation and collaboration, see Chapter 7.)

Your Turn ...

(Cover the section below and write on a note pad how you might resolve this issue.)

Here's another example of where the needs or preferences of one spouse become a priority for the other. What a unique and original way to show one's love!

It's clear to Tina that her priorities are different from Tom's. At some point it occurs to her that her biggest priority is Tom. Immediately after this affirmation, she says out loud that she "gets it." Because Tom is a priority, Tina is able to come up with a collaboration deal. After some discussion, Tom and Tina manage to work out an arrangement. Tina will play with the children when she gets home, but together with the eldest child, will begin to clean up. Tom will lower his expectations as to how clean the house should be.

TIP: Strengthen your love by collaborating.

Marriage Is Number One

A few years ago, a TV newsmagazine program focused upon the busy life of a young couple who both worked and tried to raise their children. The camera crew followed the family throughout their daily routine, starting with rising in the morning and heading off to daycare, school and work.

Later in the day when the family reunited, the crew was on hand to record their typical hectic evening. After the kids went to bed, the husband and wife poured two cups of tea and went off to the living room for a visit to discuss their day.

WHAT is happening here?

I was delighted with what I was watching. Of all the couples in the area, the TV crew chose the right one! Here was a very busy pair of young parents who had not let their work or parenting responsibilities divide them. In spite of their busy lives and feelings of exhaustion in the evening, they made their relationship a priority.

TEAM TOOLS

For a marriage to remain healthy, a couple have to set aside time regularly (daily if possible) to listen to and speak with one another. These talks are not simply information sharing, but are more personal, with feelings being expressed and shared.

Couples who have been having trouble with their relationship may be tempted to focus on "how we are doing" during the talks. One spouse, the one most worried about the future of the marriage, often feels this need more than the other. (Healthy couples don't usually talk about their marriage. Perhaps they do occasionally, but more often they just discuss the lives they live.)

When feelings are included, the conversation becomes more intimate and meaningful; even little feelings about small events are significant.

What's most important is the communication. The topic has value only because it means something to the speaker. (For more on daily talks, see Chapter 5.)

TIP: Spend time together listening and talking.

"Let's review the Tips..."

- It is OK to ask your spouse to change.

- Be honest about expectations from the get-go.

- Adjust to one another and for one another.

- Don't expect your spouse to be a mind reader.

- Marriage calls forth our potential.

- Your spouse can help you grow in confidence.

- Love by honouring the preferences of your spouse.

- Standing firm can help others confront issues from the past.

- The relationship counts, not the activity.

- Stretch into the world of the other and enhance intimacy.

- Finding time alone strengthens the bond.

- Strengthen your love by collaborating.

- Spend time together listening and talking.

CHAPTER TWO

Peace With The Past

Our attitudes, beliefs and behaviours are influenced by our history.

There is an old saying: "One who ignores history is destined to repeat it," and this couldn't be more true when it comes to relationships.

When we undertake a review of our family history, the challenge is to be as objective as possible, and to see what we can learn about ourselves. We might realize how similar or different we are to our parents or siblings, in terms of personality traits. We might also notice that our spouse seems to resemble members of our family.

An objective recollection of the past includes trying to see how everyone contributed to both good and bad times. Each family member was both strong and weak in his or her own way.

Occasionally, a family review will expose painful memories to do with abandonment, abuse, feelings of inferiority, or even death. Often in childhood, we didn't have the opportunity to openly share our thoughts and feelings. We may have believed that ignoring a hurtful memory was a good way to get rid of it. However, when feelings aren't shared and released through understanding, they may go "underground." Therefore, it can be a shock to have emotions resurface just as strongly when we start to discuss our history. Carrying around such historical "baggage" can compromise our lives in the present.

It can be helpful at such times to write an autobiography in which memories and the related feelings are described. Writing letters to parents or others from the past can be helpful as well, but it is suggested that such letters NOT be sent. It is necessary, however, to accept the accompanying upset and pain. Letting the story out and releasing the associated emotions can be a healing experience. **The past then loses its negative influence on the present.**

Significant relationships outside the family should also be discussed in a family history review. A good question to ask oneself about such li-aisons is, "What did I learn about myself from that relationship?" or "How could I have helped to make that relationship more successful?"

If we ignore the past, hoping it will simply go away, an unpleasant surprise may await us. Old habits will emerge, dancing like skeletons out of a closet. The 60% failure rate of second marriages may indicate that couples haven't learned from their past mistakes, often inno-cently made. Unless peace is made with the past, it may overshadow the present.

GINA AND GORD

Gina is shy by nature, and growing up with her parents' difficult behav-iour contributed to this personality trait. She and Gord have both been open to change, and are experiencing personal growth as a result.

Boozy Bluster

Gina loved her father very much, but she suffered greatly because of his drinking. He would come home drunk several times a week and initiate a fight with anyone available. When he was sober, he was a gentle soul and seldom said anything negative. Her mother would call the shots for the most part, and he would go along with her decisions. Also, he was very affectionate, whereas her mother was cool and standoffish.

Things changed, however, when Gina's dad drank. He would yell at Gina's mother, criticize her ideas, and lash out at the kids for no particular reason. Gina found her home life pleasant in many ways, and yet scary at the same time, as she knew the effects that alcohol had on her father's behaviour.

WHAT *happened here?*

Gina was confused. She had a strong bond with her father, as he was warm and affectionate in contrast to her more emotionally reserved mother. She valued the relationship, but couldn't trust it, as her father would be transformed when he drank. At these times he was distant and mean, and this was hurtful to Gina.

Gina's mother was more consistent, but controlling and cold. Gina came away from her family experience with a tendency not to trust anyone because of her erratic relationship with her father. She also resented anyone who seemed to be trying to control her.

TEAM TOOLS

Abuse in childhood can create wounds with effects that linger. If Gina hopes to have a successful marriage, it would help to make peace with her past. Talking with Gord or her friends or seeing a therapist would be a good way to start. These people can be witnesses to past pain and ease the suffering of Gina by allowing her to have these experiences validated.

Gina can also do some writing and discover that she can identify and release old feelings. She may be surprised at the intensity of her emotions when writing about her past memories. It could be that when the actual events occurred she was forced to suppress the associated feelings.

Making peace with the past:

Gina decides to see a psychologist so that she can better understand her family history and the impact it had upon her. She relives some of her memories and becomes upset as she recalls the troubled times she had with her parents. She writes each of them a letter, which allows her to focus on each of them independently.

These letters provoke rich and painful feelings. (Gina doesn't send the letters to her parents.) She also talks with a couple of good friends who, in turn, discuss their own histories with her. Gina finds that her ability to trust improves and her sensitivity to control lightens up.

TIP: Discussing memories and the feelings that go with them can be liberating.

Super Sensitive

Gina and Gord have two children and are functioning fairly well. Gina is determined to parent her children somewhat differently from the way she was raised. She and Gord collaborate well in this area.

There is an area of sensitivity, however, for Gina. Gord is not much of a drinker, but at parties he will have a beer, sometimes two. Gina watches Gord carefully, and when he has a second beer, she becomes agitated and comments on his drinking. Such feedback doesn't go well with Gord, as he also had a controlling parent and doesn't like to be told what to do. Sometimes, if he becomes annoyed, he will have a third drink to prove to Gina that he's his own man. She then becomes even more upset and an argument ensues.

WHAT is happening here?

Gina never had a face-to-face talk with her father about their life as a family and her feelings about the way his behaviour changed when he drank. She didn't want to upset him. Gina thought that her previous counselling sessions had dealt with this aspect of her life. Her father's death the previous year, however, may have triggered further hurt that wasn't explored in her therapy sessions.

TEAM TOOLS

It has been mentioned previously that unresolved issues from the past may interfere with the present. This is confusing for Gina, as she thought she had left her past hurts behind. Some of the old pain was probably released, but she still needs to review her history once more and pay special attention to her father's drinking and its impact upon her.

Making peace with the past:

Gina writes another letter about all the things she liked and missed, as well as her hurt and embarrassment with her father's drinking. This writing provokes a lot of tears and anger, and in the end, she is able to forgive her father for his failings. After going through this debriefing process, Gina discovers strengths garnered from her history, and compassion for others' struggles, as well as her own. She also loses much of her sensitivity to Gord's social drinking.

TIP: Issues from the past can colour the present.

JOAN AND JOHN

Joan and John are attempting to deepen their relationship. Joan knows that it's important to go through this process, as she doesn't want to repeat the problems of her first marriage. She knows from her parents' experience that healthy dialogue is crucial to the success of any marriage.

Objectivity Obtained

When Joan was a child, her mother could become irritable when she was tired and her father would shut down. The more irritable her mother got, the more her father shut down; the more her father shut down, the more irritable her mother became. Joan's dad didn't like conflict and would try to avoid it if possible. Her mother liked to talk things out to reach some sort of conclusion, not minding if tempers flared. Sometimes she didn't realize that she was yelling.

Joan's dad could get angry as well, and would at times speak up, but generally he would withdraw and brood. Joan's sister was an "accomplished pouter" and this behaviour bothered Joan, but she didn't realize until she was older that her father did the same thing.

WHAT *happened here?*

Joan's parents had a set pattern of communication. Although there were periods of harmony, an atmosphere of conflict was more often the norm. Joan was convinced for the longest time in her teen years that her mother was the problem because she was too temperamental and aggressive at times. Unlike her father, Joan wouldn't withdraw, but instead, challenged her mother. They often clashed, and this contributed to her sense that her mother was the problem parent.

TEAM TOOLS

It's important to realize that both parents (or caregivers) often took turns playing the roles of "hero" or "villain."

A serious illness often shakes up a family and changes long-held patterns of communication. When Joan's father became ill, her understanding of her parents' relationship changed.

Making peace with the past:

Joan's father was diagnosed with lung cancer. He underwent major surgery and had one of his lungs removed. He nearly died during the surgery, and his heart was compromised. This brush with death transformed Joan's father in that he became braver and spoke up in situations where he had withdrawn in the past. He was able to debate with Joan's mother, and this actually calmed her down. As a result, they were better able to resolve their issues.

With her father's change in behaviour, Joan realized that he had been part of the problem with regard to her parents' tension and conflict. He would withdraw when tired and not talk to her mother, who hungered for interaction. He might do things behind her back so as not to aggravate her, and would end up annoying her more and wounding the trust between them. From time to time, he would erupt in his own anger and cause family upsets. Joan neither saw these behaviours nor realized their impact until her father nearly died.

TIP: *Try to recall your past with objectivity.*

KEN AND KIM

Introduction: Ken is reserved and doesn't like fighting. He was exposed to a lot of conflict within his birth family and it left him sensitive to arguments in his relationship with Kim.

Too Much Fighting

Ken's parents argued on a regular basis. They were both working full-time while trying to raise a family, and their fatigue and money worries led to frequent blow-ups. Ken and his sister would escape to their rooms and wait for things to settle down. Sometimes the fights would escalate and objects would be thrown; Ken would be fearful that someone might get hurt. He also worried that his parents might break up and divorce.

Kim is an energetic and expressive woman who can be openly angry. She also had parents who scrapped a lot and she feels it's normal for her to assertively voice her concerns. Ken dislikes Kim's anger and will back down if something upsetting is discussed.

WHAT *is happening here?*

Ken has come away from his birth family with a sensitivity to fighting. He had an ample dose of it when he was a kid and never wants to fight in his own marriage. Interestingly enough, his wife Kim also had a volatile home life, but for her, arguing is part of a normal family life.

TEAM TOOLS

Parents who fight regularly distress their children, who then, as adults, may fear any kind of confrontation. If Ken doesn't overcome his sensitivity to arguing with Kim, his marriage is going to be negatively affected.

If on the other hand, he is open to finding constructive ways to disagree and resolve issues, he will discover that he's not repeating his parents' experience.

Making peace with the past:

Ken: *"It bothers me that you made plans with your parents."*
Kim: *"What's the big deal? We haven't seen them for weeks."*
Ken: *"What if I had some ideas for Sunday afternoon?"*
Kim: *"You didn't say anything about plans of your own."*

Ken: *"Well it frustrates me when you don't consult."*

Kim: *"I hear your annoyance. I wasn't trying to exclude you."*

Ken: *"I realize that, but it still bugs me."*

Kim: *"Do you want me to call them and make some changes?"*

Ken: *"No, no. Let's go ahead. You're right, it has been awhile."*

TIP: It is possible to resolve differences constructively.

Flat Marriage Syndrome

Ken has decided to seek out a counsellor to discuss his marriage to Kim. He tells the therapist that he loves Kim, but that he doesn't feel "in love" with her, and that he's considering leaving the relationship.

When asked what things bother him about his wife or the marriage, Ken replies that because he is easy going, very little bothers him about Kim. When asked if he is able to tell Kim that he's frustrated at times, he says he doesn't like to hurt her feelings, and therefore, keeps his complaints to himself. "Besides," he says, "They're no big deal."

WHAT is happening here?

Ken believes it's important to feel in love with his spouse, and because his feelings are flat, he wonders about staying together. Ken grew up in a home where his mother was depressed and frequently upset about even the smallest of concerns. He became very sensitive about upsetting her and would keep his worries to himself in an attempt to protect his mother.

TEAM TOOLS

When feelings go flat, some couples consider ending their relationship instead of figuring out what's wrong and making the necessary repairs. Such reactions may lead these couples to give up too easily when troubles arise.

Ken is very easy-going and may unintentionally be hurting his relationship. He is sensitive to upsetting other people, and therefore, holds back his frustrations from Kim. There is a connection between his withheld emotion and his "flat" love feelings. If Ken is going to feel in love with his wife, he has to be open with her about his concerns.

Making peace with the past:

Ken and Kim have been trying T-Times (see Chapter 4) and in the process, have opened up dialogue about various issues. Kim has always been candid, but is now also giving some attention to the impact of her words upon Ken.

For his part, Ken is now more open about what annoys him, and Kim is receptive to the feedback. Ken is feeling that his marriage is being rejuvenated. He now says that he feels "in love" with the woman he loves.

TIP: Share your full range of emotions.

OLIVIA

Olivia is independent, but has done well stretching into some of Ossie's interests. He has reciprocated, and this has strengthened their marriage.

Dump the Parents

Olivia has many leftover issues regarding her relationship with her mother. The two of them clashed a lot when Olivia was a teenager, and didn't manage to work out a good reconciliation. Their relationship was fine for a time, but after Olivia had her second child, she distanced herself from her mother and father. She no longer speaks with them and also withholds contact with the two grandchildren.

WHAT happened here?

It's not uncommon for parents and children to clash. Often these difficulties are resolved over time with improved maturity all around. In this situation, Olivia has chosen to manage her anger and hurt by cutting herself and her children off from her parents.

TEAM TOOLS

Cutting off contact with a family member as a means of resolving old hurts is unfortunate and short-sighted. Nothing is improved or changed for the better by creating new wounds. As the old saying goes, "Two wrongs do not make a right."

Olivia is robbing her own children of a relationship with their grandparents. She is also setting a poor example for her children in terms of solving problems with parents. It would be more mature to sit down with her mother and discuss old concerns in an attempt to move beyond them.

Making peace with the past:

Olivia's mother goes to see a psychologist to discuss her upset with the lack of relationship with her daughter and grandchildren. Her mother is grieving the loss of these connections and feeling a lot of distress as well. The therapist suggests that Olivia attend some sessions, and Olivia agrees to do so.

The first meeting is with Olivia and the psychologist to develop rapport and talk about options. Olivia is angry and upset about old hurts, but is agreeable to finally discussing them openly in the next session. This meeting is candid and emotional, and a bridge is built between mother and daughter.

TIP: *Cutting off contact doesn't resolve old hurts.*

ROSA AND RON

Introduction: Rosa and Ron have been dating for a couple of years. Ron is talkative and somewhat assertive, and Rosa is more introverted. This couple have been doing well in their relationship, and Ron is beginning to think about marriage.

Getting Close is Scary

Ron and Rosa are getting to the point where a deeper commitment seems to make sense to Ron. He broaches the topic with Rosa, and she becomes quiet and distant. Ron is upset. He feels betrayed by Rosa and angrily tells her so. Rosa continues to withdraw, and Ron ends the evening abruptly.

WHAT *is happening here*?

Ron and Rosa love each other and have been growing closer. Ron is thinking about proposing marriage, but thinks it would be a good idea to talk in general terms first. He's anxious about doing this, as he has sensed some reluctance on Rosa's part.

Rosa loves Ron but she hasn't let herself think about the future. It scares her. Her parents broke up when she was ten, and she recalls the pain it caused her and her brothers. She is harbouring a secret fear of marriage that she hasn't mentioned to Ron. When he raises the future so directly, she freezes and withdraws. She feels guilty about Ron's upset feelings, but her fear of commitment is deep.

TEAM TOOLS

When someone has experienced a big loss in childhood and it was not discussed openly at the time, it can be scary to commit to a relationship as an adult.

It is important to find out what's going on below the surface. Sometimes, after a negative response to an issue, it's necessary to ask some questions—particularly about feelings, and to allow the whole story to unfold.

If Ron reacts negatively towards Rosa instead of being open, they might not be able to work through the underlying issues. It's important to explore the past, as this step can begin the healing of old wounds. Rosa was hurt by her parents' divorce. She may be afraid of marriage, but by sharing these feelings and moving ahead cautiously, she will find herself becoming less fearful and more confident.

The dialogue below illustrates a gentler and more effective approach to discussing and resolving Rosa's fear of marriage.

Ron: *"I've been thinking about us and wondering about the future."*
Rosa: *(sits quietly with her eyes averted)*
Ron: *"Does this topic make you uncomfortable, Sweetheart?"*
Rosa: *"It scares me to death. I keep thinking of all the trouble my parents had and how their marriage ended."*
Ron: *"Are you afraid that history will repeat itself?"*
Rosa: *"I know it's crazy. I feel so guilty because I know I'm hurting you by being standoffish."*
Ron: *"I thought you didn't care for me enough. I don't like to see you scared, but now that I know the reason, I'm relieved."*

TIP: Make peace with the past and live a happier life in the present.

Big Loss Buried

Eleven year-old Rosa came home from school one day and found her aunt and uncle sitting in the living room talking quietly and sadly with her mother. Her mother looked extremely upset. Rosa was unnerved and worried, but her aunt and uncle and mother ignored her.

Her younger brother, Davey, beckoned her to follow him into a bedroom. He closed the door and told Rosa that their father had just died. Rosa started sobbing and hugged Davey. Their mother and the other relatives never did discuss her father's sudden death with her.

WHAT *happened here?*

Rosa suffered a tremendous loss in the death of her father. She was only in grade six at the time and felt abandoned once again, as she was still recovering from her parents' divorce. What made things worse was that everyone avoided talking with her, and for the most part, with each other, about her father. It was as if he never existed. This conspiracy of silence made things much more difficult for Rosa.

In later years, Rosa was very closed emotionally and prone to depression around the time of year that her father died. She also had trouble building close relationships with men, as she deeply feared that they would abandon her as well.

TEAM TOOLS

Discussing losses openly or writing about them can help to prevent long-term problems. Rosa's family dealt with her father's sudden death in the way they believed would be most helpful.

For many years, it was thought that ignoring big losses was the best way to manage them. We now know that this only pushes the grief "underground." The unresolved grief can contribute to mental health problems such as depression or anxiety conditions, along with fear of commitment.

Making peace with the past:

Rosa is in counselling and her focus is on her family. She's writing her autobiography and it has taken her back to the time when her father suddenly died. She's feeling the same fear and sadness she felt as a young girl. She wasn't able to talk about this pain when she was a child, as no one took the time to listen to her. Through her writing and conversations with Ron, her psychologist, and a few select friends, she's feeling more at ease and developing closer bonds.

TIP: Sharing sad feelings is painful but healthy.

SUSAN AND STAN

Introduction: Susan and Stan have been struggling in their marriage, which is the second for both of them. This has made Susan even more protective of her children than she would be normally. She also has memories of growing up with a mother who was an alcoholic.

Protective Avoidance

Susan has decided to have no contact with her mother because she is an alcoholic and Susan doesn't wish to expose her two children to someone who is addicted in this way. Susan remembers how hard it was to grow up in a home with her mother drinking frequently. She was embarrassed and wouldn't bring friends home to play. She reluctantly withdraws contact with her mother so as to protect her children.

WHAT *is happening here?*

Susan has lived with her mother's alcoholism for a long time and uses her children as an excuse not to see her any more. She hasn't come to this decision easily. She only retreats after some visits where her mother behaved erratically in front of her grandchildren, which confused and upset them. Susan tells Stan that she feels some guilt and sadness at not being able to have regular contact with her parents.

TEAM TOOLS

Avoiding a parent because of their addiction may seem sensible, particularly when young children are involved. However, it may be possible to create another solution if the addicted parent will cooperate. This will allow the family to still have contact, but in a way that is pleasant and positive.

Your Turn...

(Cover the section below and write on a note pad how you might resolve this issue.)

Making peace with the past:

Susan attended a counselling session with the intention of discussing the upset and guilt she felt about her relationship with her alcoholic mother. She spent some time dealing with her old hurts and angers, and was able to move to a place of forgiveness. She then developed a plan, which she presented to her mother. Susan told her that she would only visit if she didn't drink. If she chose to drink during a visit, Susan and her family would leave and visit again another day.

Her mother was annoyed at first and angry with the proposal, but quickly settled down and agreed to the terms. She was upset with not having had much contact with her grandchildren or Susan and Stan.

The first visit went well. During the second visit, her mother poured herself a glass of wine, and Susan gathered up her children, reminded her mother of the terms of their agreement, and left. There has been no further drinking during visits.

TIP: Creative problem solving is better than abandonment.

TINA AND TOM

Tom and Tina are committed parents of three children and have been able to find time to talk with each other on a regular basis. They have learned to collaborate around parenting issues. However, Tina is less open with her thoughts and feelings than Tom. She learned to be this way as a child.

No Objectivity

Tina's parents fought frequently when she lived at home. She blamed her dad for most of the trouble. Her dad was frequently a cranky man with a tendency to criticize everyone who crossed his path.

Her mom would react passively by withdrawing during negative exchanges. She would sulk and not talk to anyone for days. This frightened and upset Tina. She worried that she might be the problem, as her mother closed her out, along with her dad.

WHAT happened here?

Tina was exposed to her parents' poor communication patterns on a regular basis. There were times when things went well with her mom and dad. At other times when things deteriorated and the old pattern would repeat itself, it seemed to Tina that the major culprit was her father. She knew that her mother's withdrawals were upsetting, and she blamed her father for this behaviour as well.

TEAM TOOLS

An outspoken and temperamental parent can easily be blamed as the source of poor communication in a marriage. It's not hard to understand why Tina would conclude that her father's behaviour was the main problem within her parents' relationship. Her dad could get irritable, especially when he was tired or distressed.

On the other hand, Tina's mother was a reactionary listener, and instead of focusing on her husband's mood and attempting to discuss it with him, she felt discomfort and withdrew. In turn, Tina's dad would feel upset by his wife's withdrawing and sulking for long periods. He would want to resolve an issue, but his wife would avoid him. He would then feel abandoned, and Tina's mother would feel angry and overwhelmed. No one knew how to talk it out.

It can be useful for Tina and Tom to take some time to review their family histories. They can discuss their memories or write about them, and then talk. It's important to also note and discuss the feelings that accompany the memories. This process helps to create some objectivity about the past.

Making peace with the past:

When Tina and Tom got married, Tina was hopeful that she wouldn't repeat her parents' communication patterns. During their courtship, the talking and listening went well for the most part. After being married for about a year, some difficulties began to arise. Tom would become upset and temperamental, and Tina found herself withdrawing, as her mother used to do.

Recognizing that they may be repeating parental patterns, Tom and Tina have now decided to spend some time talking about their family histories and actually writing down some of their memories. They write not only the memory, but also the feelings that went along with the memory.

Tina is able to write and discuss her old upset with her father's temper and her mother's withdrawal. She recalls that she was fearful of her father, and that at times, she feels the same way with Tom. This helps Tom to better understand what might be happening for Tina when she withdraws.

TIP: History need not repeat itself.

"Let's review the Tips..."

• Discussing memories and the feelings that go with them can be liberating.

• Issues from the past can colour the present.

• Try to recall your past objectively.

• It is possible to resolve differences constructively.

• Share your full range of emotions.

• Cutting off contact doesn't resolve old hurts.

• Make peace with the past and live a happier life in the present.

• Sharing sad feelings is painful but healthy.

• Creative problem solving is better than abandonment.

• History need not repeat itself.

CHAPTER THREE

Unconditional Love

Love is often a misunderstood and maligned concept in our culture. Love is much more than warm fuzzy feelings; it is an act of the will, or an action to be taken. Love is meant to be given away from one person and received by another.

To love unconditionally means to give at all times. If a husband is discouraged, he's more likely to change his attitude or release his feelings if his wife continues to love and to be positive. If, however, she decides to play "tit for tat," it only causes greater problems. Feeling loved can help him want to change and improve. Feeling criticized, however, can lead to defensiveness and a tendency to become more entrenched in a negative attitude or behaviour.

To love unconditionally requires commitment and a willingness to always place the needs of your spouse or the relationship above your own. Not just when you feel like doing it or when you think you will get something in return. The exception to this rule would be a relationship where there is abuse. To allow a spouse to be abusive isn't loving behaviour, but rather, a fearful attempt to appease or accommodate, and will only lead to further abuse.

To love unconditionally, each spouse continues loving even when the other acts in a negative way. To love means to be there for the mate in the way they need you to be. Therefore, if there is a difference of opinion leading to a heated exchange of words, there is no threat to dissolve the relationship because of the problem. There is an understanding that the commitment is sound and won't be suddenly revoked. The choice is to be together – miserably or happily – but together. Such an attitude leads to an obvious outcome. Who wants to be together and be miserable?

To love unconditionally means to respect differences. In order to facilitate harmonious living, certain changes can be requested, as mentioned in Chapter 1 ("Attitude"). However, it's tempting at times to want the other person to change too much. It seems to be a human tendency to try and remake the other person in our own image!

To love unconditionally is to give without self-interest. A conditional lover, on the other hand, gives just 50% (and often less), and only if the other partner does her part. If the spouse stops pulling her share of the load, so does the conditional lover. Also, there's a threat, which is seldom far away, that the relationship may end if the other doesn't behave in the manner expected.

To love unconditionally leads to a healthy conclusion. Even if the other doesn't respond in kind (which the conditional lover would expect), there's a sense of well-being. Loving your spouse in this way leads to peace and personal growth. Conversely, to love with self-interest with no results can lead to resentment and frustration.

Human beings who give of themselves with no self-interest seem to benefit from the experience. "The Helper's High" is the term given to the feeling experienced by those who reach out to others unconditionally, and appears to be related to an endorphin release. It's as if the body is built to love unconditionally!

Self Love is Misdirected and Overrated!

In a recent radio interview, the creator of a dating service stated that he requires that his clients "love themselves" before he will work with them. He then added the common adage "You can't love another unless you first love yourself." I, however, believe that the ability to love is derived from other sources.

Children develop a sound self-concept if their attachment needs are met early on in their development. The love of a parent or caregiver supports and affirms the identity of the child. If attachment needs, however, are overlooked or ignored, a child may experience a wounded self-concept. He may doubt his worth and become self-critical or self-demeaning.

Woundedness created by inadequate love from another cannot be corrected by trying to "love oneself." If our woundedness results from breakdowns in our early attachments, it makes sense that love from another person will be necessary to make the correction. Love is an action word, flowing from one person to another, and in its pure form, heals the giver and the receiver. Yet popular psychology is fond of prescribing the self-love quick fix.

Self-love proponents are quick to say that there's a difference between self-love and selfishness. However, it may be difficult to separate the two. We are born very self-centered and need to be so in order to survive. Our own fundamental needs are our entire focus. But unless we develop a social conscience and awareness, we can grow up to be self-centered adults.

If we're feeling discouraged, becoming more self-centered is not likely to help. Discouragement may even be the result of being too self-occupied. Trying to bolster a discouraged self-concept by becoming our own greatest fan may not be as effective as hoped, and could unintentionally feed our selfish side.

How about considering self-awareness of strengths and weaknesses instead of self-love? What if we consider self-acceptance of those strengths and weaknesses and making changes where desired or needed?

Buddhism teaches "No Self, No Problem." When a person is detached from himself, he is free from the problems associated with self absorption. Christianity teaches that a person who seeks his life will lose it, and he who loses his life for the sake of love will find it. Christianity also says to love our neighbour as we love ourselves; however, this is interpreted by the self-love crowd as permission to be great self-lovers. The teaching doesn't say to love yourself and then your neighbour. It says love your neighbour. How? The way you already love yourself! Self-love is a given.

Self-confidence and happiness/joy are paradoxical. If one is detached and forgets oneself and loves without counting the cost (unconditionally), there is resulting peace and joy. If one loves and "keeps score," there may be unhappiness and discouragement if expectations aren't satisfied. When a person is preoccupied with self pep-talk, there may be some payoff, but not peace or joy.

The dating service fellow matches people in love with themselves, who as a result, may have trouble making their relationships work. A great marriage is made up of two people who are able to "be there" for each other. Good listening and consultation, and most importantly, collaboration, are necessary for success. The ideas or preferences of the other person have to be as important as one's own, if not more so at times.

A reactionary listener is someone who is self-focused to the point where he hears his own reaction rather than the feeling or idea of the other person. In marital counselling, we work hard to break down this self-focus so that each spouse can "hear" the other better.

It's not possible to work out all of one's insecurities before marriage, as some of them only show up after the wedding. It's what happens between the couple that determines the success of the relationship, not how much each partner loves him or herself. Being with a spouse awakens old attachment issues from childhood, and presents the opportunity to heal the wounds of the past.

Self-worth or esteem is not a prerequisite for intimacy, but rather, the result of it. In other words, if two people contribute to a healthy relationship and grow accordingly, even if something happens to one of them, the personal growth and self-confidence will remain in spite of the pain suffered in the loss.

Self-love is indeed misdirected and overrated!

BOB AND BETH

As newly weds, Bob and Beth enjoy spending time with one another and are learning to collaborate.

Helpful Son Spurned

Bob's parents are thinking about buying some new furniture. He offers to do some research for them, and they both accept. He goes on-line and downloads several pages of material, which he delivers to his parents. His mother shows some interest and his father ignores the information and decides to do something quite different from what Bob thought. Bob becomes angry and storms out of a family dinner.

WHAT is *happening here?*

Bob likes to help his parents. When his father accepts his offer to help and then ignores it, Bob feels some frustration and disappointment. He's also offended that his parents aren't taking advantage of the work he did on their behalf. He had expected them to be grateful and to have used his research.

TEAM TOOLS

It can be tempting to give a gift and to expect some positive feedback. If the feedback comes, all is well and good. If the feedback doesn't come and the giver is offended, then the gift wasn't unconditional. If Bob had given the gift freely, with no expectations, he wouldn't have been as upset. The nature of an expectation can be readily determined by discussing it with a spouse.

If there's a history of this sort of behaviour by the parents, it would be appropriate to talk with them about it. In this situation, the parents' ignoring their son's advice is a rarity, which makes it more difficult for Bob to accept.

Loving unconditionally:

When Bob next visits his parents, there's still some awkwardness remaining from their last encounter. Bob, however, has come to realize that he needs to accept his father's right to do what he wants with the information he provided. Bob notices the new furniture his parents have bought and he compliments them on their choice.

TIP: *Give freely!*

HANNA AND HARVEY

This couple have been open to growth and have influenced each other in many positive ways. They like to spend time together, and embrace each other's interests.

Power Shift

Harvey and Hanna are good at finding half an hour together each day to chat, and as a result, both are listening more effectively to each other.

They are currently visiting friends in another city, but have gone out for a walk so as to talk privately. Hanna is upset because she's just had a phone conversation with her mother. Her mother is aging and suffers from some memory lapses. She has accused Hanna of not telling her that she was leaving town. Hanna is feeling guilty and is explaining her upset to Harvey. Harvey tells her to shake it off. He reminds her that her mother is suffering from dementia and need not be taken seriously. Hanna still feels upset.

WHAT *is happening here?*

This couple are wisely making time to get away by themselves to have a talk. Such a gesture is a statement of how much they love each other and value their relationship. Hanna is hurting because of the accusations from her mother, and has essentially given her power away. She is allowing her mother, who is several thousand kilometers away, to negatively colour her day. Harvey is giving advice instead of listening.

TEAM TOOLS

Perhaps the hardest person to listen to is one's spouse. Why is this the case? Well, each mate is intimately connected to the other and is therefore vulnerable.

The second hardest person to listen to is a parent, as old listening patterns can kick in, regardless of our intentions. When we react to another person, we stop listening and slip into a sort of self-focused rumination about what has happened. In so doing, it allows the other person's mood to control us.

Loving unconditionally:

Harvey is concerned for Hanna, as he can see that she's feeling down. His temptation is to tell her again not to let her mother bother her so much. He realizes his own discomfort is causing these thoughts to rise within him.

Harvey wants to show love for his wife and so he validates and accepts her upset. He realizes that Hanna has allowed her mother to upset her, but now he tunes into her mood, and she acknowledges this. Hanna then seems to regain her power, as she is able to sense her mother's feelings. Harvey's listening well to Hanna has freed her up to hear her mother.

Hanna can now see that her mother is upset and annoyed because she misses her. Her mother may also be embarrassed to admit that she's forgotten about the trip. Suddenly, Hanna is feeling upbeat again, and they move on to other topics.

TIP: Listen without giving away your power.

Seeing with New Eyes

Later in the summer, Hanna and Harvey are visiting Harvey's parents. They are out for a "Walk'n Talk" when Harvey asks Hanna how the visit is going. She says that it's not so good for her, and Harvey asks why. Hanna mentions some things Harvey's mother has done and said that upset her.

Harvey is surprised and tells Hanna not to worry about it, as his mother does that sort of thing all the time, and it's no big deal. He ignores such behaviour, as he has become used to it over the years. Hanna begins to cry, and Harvey tells her again to "shake it off."

WHAT is happening here?

It's easy for Harvey to make light of what's has happened, as he has dealt with his mother's behaviour in the past by ignoring it or minimizing it. In spite of his suggestions, his wife becomes more upset and Harvey starts to get frustrated.

TEAM TOOLS

It's easy to get stuck in one's own "frame of reference" when listening. Such a stance prevents the listener from really hearing the concerns of the speaker. The listener remains trapped in himself and is unable to show love by listening well.

An unconditional listener will break out of his own frame of reference and allow himself to enter into the world of the speaker. Such a step opens up a new reality for the listener, and the speaker feels heard, i.e. loved unconditionally.

Loving unconditionally:

Harvey is taken aback by Hanna's tears and realizes that she's not only frustrated and upset with his mother, but that his advice is only making things worse. In that moment, he begins to see his mother as Hanna sees her, and he understands why Hanna is upset. He may be used to his mother's moods and occasional rudeness, but Hanna isn't, and she has a right to be hurt. Harvey realizes that the time has come for him to see his mother through "new eyes" so as to help make their visits more enjoyable for his wife.

TIP: *Your frame of reference can be a trap.*

SUSAN AND STAN

Susan and Stan have been with each other now for fifteen years, but have recently gone through a breakdown in their relationship; separating for a month. Tension levels remain high.

The Blame Game

Stan and Susan are attending marriage counselling. They are both very frustrated with each other and spend much of the session pointing out the faults and poor behaviours of the other person. This is a second marriage for both Susan and Stan, and they are feeling disappointed and frustrated by their troubles.

The therapist attempts to guide the two of them away from attacking each other and encourages them to look at their own behaviours. Stan and Susan persist in their blaming. At the beginning of the next visit, they tell the therapist that they don't think they are improving, and the last session was a waste of time. Now they are blaming the therapist for their lack of progress.

WHAT is happening here?

This couple is struggling. They are both frustrated and scared, as this is their second marriage and they want it to work out well. Attempts to guide them away from playing the "Blame Game" are fruitless. The therapist gives them some ideas to try to avoid conflict such as the "Time-Out/Time-In" technique (see Chapter 8).

TEAM TOOLS

When people blame each other, they are focusing on the faults or behaviours of the other person and ignoring their own role. Such behaviour implies that the blamer is superior or more important, and that the other should smarten up. This isn't helpful for either party.

An unconditional lover will take responsibility for his part in a dispute (see Step Four in Time-Out/Time-In). Such insight stops the blaming and opens up healing dialogue. Stan and Susan were partly justified in blaming the counsellor, who focused too much on teaching and not enough on the mutual hurt of the spouses. Sometimes, however, a couple are locked into playing the "The Blame Game" and will blame the therapist regardless of what he does, rather than taking individual responsibility for change.

Loving unconditionally:

Susan and Stan are disappointed and frustrated that they have been having trouble. The therapist focuses on their moods and tries to hear the various feelings of each person. Instead of refocusing the blame, he spends time on the feelings behind the attacks, and Stan and Susan begin to feel less defensive. The therapist then offers some ideas about how to manage their problems differently, and Susan and Stan are more open to the suggestions.

TIP: Blaming blinds a person to his own faults.

Tit for Tat

Susan and Stan decide to put together a chore contract. Each one now has a list of duties and time frames in which to carry them out. Because they both work, an equal sharing of tasks is important. This arrangement works well for a time. At a certain point, Susan doesn't complete her chores at the allotted time. Stan notices, but doesn't say much because he can see that Susan is tired. When the same thing happens again the next week, he speaks up, and Susan becomes upset with him. Stan becomes frustrated and stops doing his chores. Susan isn't impressed and goes "on strike."

WHAT is happening here?

Susan and Stan are trying to share the responsibilities of running their home. They have written up a contract with each of their duties outlined. When Susan doesn't follow through with some of her chores, it causes upset for Stan. He has been monitoring her performance and allowing his own efforts to be determined by Susan's efforts or lack thereof. If she does her jobs, he will do his, and vice versa.

TEAM TOOLS

Contracts can be seen as a sincere attempt to organize work schedules within a home. The danger is that they can also lead to "conditional love." If the contract commitments are meant to structure work schedules, there can be a benefit. If, however, the contract leads to keeping score, it has become a conditional love tool and loses its effectiveness.

Let's revisit this scene with unconditional love thrown in:

Susan and Stan are following a contract and this arrangement works well for a time. At a certain point, Susan doesn't complete her chores at the allotted time. Stan notices but doesn't say much because he can see that Susan is tired. He asks her if she's tired, and she says she is. He offers to help her with her chores, and she accepts. When she's tired again, he also talks with her and listens to her concerns about her work commitments. She feels energized and gets on with her duties.

TIP: Unconditional lovers do not keep score.

Positive Tit for Tat

Stan and Susan are continuing to see a psychologist for their relationship issues. In one of the sessions, Stan talks with the therapist about Susan, outlining her faults, and expressing upset and discouragement about their situation as a couple. He realizes that he has been acting poorly as a way of getting back at his wife, and that his behaviour has not inspired her to improve in any way. In fact, she is becoming more distant with each day that passes.

WHAT is happening here?

Stan is reacting to Susan's faults by responding in kind. Traditionally, he has avoided conflict by keeping his concerns to himself. Even though he has been more outspoken lately, he hasn't been talking with Susan about his concerns because they seldom talk in depth.

TEAM TOOLS

Talking openly about concerns can be an excellent way to resolve misunderstandings. Attitude also plays a role. Stan is trying to relay a message to Susan and it is not working.

The therapist suggests that he try a different approach: be friendly to Susan regardless of what she does, and fulfill his own commitments.

Loving unconditionally:

Stan has decided to be pleasant and friendly with Susan in spite of his upset with her. He continues to be concerned with various aspects of the relationship, but he's not allowing these issues to control his behaviour.

They come for another counselling session, and both of them look lighter and happier. The therapist asks Susan how she's doing, as she appears upbeat and positive. She says that things have been going well between her and Stan, and that it's easy to be positive because Stan has been so nice to her.

TIP: Kindness begets kindness.

TOM AND TINA

Tom and Tina are still finding time for each other and have been building good will through their talks. They both remain dedicated parents.

Baby as Teacher

Tom and Tina's fourteen-month-old son, Conor, still occasionally wakes up in the middle of the night. During these times, he calls out for his father, who wakes at the sound of his name. Realizing that he needs to be refreshed for work in the morning, Tom nudges Tina, who stumbles out of bed to attend to their son. Conor, however, still wants his dad, and calls out even louder. Tom pretends to be asleep, and feels mildly guilty for not responding.

WHAT is happening here?

Mothers tend to be the ones who get up in the night with their children, and Tom justifies his support of this trend by telling himself he needs his rest. He believes that he's too tired to get out of bed and comfort his son. Tina is a good sport, and tries to spend time with Conor, even though he becomes more agitated and calls for his father.

TEAM TOOLS

There is a common misperception that a person can only love if they "feel like" doing so. When a person is tired, it can be tempting to withdraw and not attend to the needs of those close to us. Loving is not tied to the emotional state of the lover. Granted, it can be easier to love if one feels loving, but most mothers will tell you that it's possible to love even if the emotional inclination is not present. Love takes willpower.

Loving unconditionally:

Conor greets his mother with upset, and calls out louder for his daddy. Tom decides to get out of bed and go to his son's room. He comforts Conor, but in a hurried and perfunctory manner, and finds his way back to bed. His son settles and seems to nod off to sleep again.

A few moments later, Conor begins to once again call his father. Tom listens for a time, hoping the boy will settle, but the calls become louder. Tom rolls out of bed again and heads for Conor's room, and this time he decides he will try to be friendlier and gentler with his son. This isn't easy to do because of his feelings of fatigue and frustration.

Tom hears the pleasant tones of his own voice, which is a contrast to what he feels inside. He gives his son a hug and chats with him a bit, changes his diaper again, and kisses him goodnight. Conor goes to sleep. Tom returns to bed feeling calmer and falls asleep quickly.

MORE TEAM TOOLS

Tom goes through an attitude change and decides to be as loving as he can towards his little boy. This decision is a pure act of will, as he is feeling out of sorts. It's almost as if Conor wants his dad to come and take care of him whether he feels like it or not, but also to be positive about the experience. When Tom fulfills this unvoiced expectation of his son, Conor settles immediately, and so does Tom when he returns to bed. Later, Tom marvels about the lesson he has learned from his fourteen-month-old son: **It is possible to love regardless of how you feel and it is important to express this love well!**

TIP: *Love with your willpower.*

VERONICA AND VINCE

Introduction: Veronica and Vince have been married for several years. Veronica is a long suffering appeaser. She believes that to love unconditionally means to ignore bad behaviour and make excuses for it at the same time. Unfortunately, her husband Vince misses out on invaluable feedback that might help him change for the better.

Is This Unconditional Love?

Veronica has been trying hard to love her husband. She finds him moody and negative much of the time, and she bends over backwards to try and make him happy. She realizes that when he yells, he is tired, and she excuses him for his negativity. When he's late or drinks too much, she makes other excuses for him. Veronica dislikes conflict or hurting feelings, and tries to avoid volatile situations.

She comes to a point where she can't continue, and leaves Vince for a few days. He is shocked and wants to repair things, but it may be too late for Veronica. She has put up with his poor behaviour long enough. She tells a friend that "unconditional love doesn't work."

WHAT *is happening here?*

Veronica believes that she's showing love for her husband by being a long suffering wife. She tries hard to see things his way, and makes excuses for his poor behaviour. She admits that she doesn't like conflict or hurt feelings, and in doing so, she tips her hand. Veronica isn't loving her spouse; she's loving herself.

TEAM TOOLS

Unconditional love involves loving another person with no conditions attached, i.e. expecting no love in return. Even when the other person doesn't return the love, the person who is loving unconditionally still feels happy and peaceful.

If, on the other hand, she feels resentful or angry at the lack of a positive response, her love hasn't been unconditional, but rather, conditional. In Veronica's case, her love was conditional in that she expected a payoff, which was peace at all costs. To really love Vince unconditionally, she needs to love in a way that is beneficial to him, even though it may cause initial upset and upheaval.

Loving unconditionally:

Vince has been trying to open up more since his wake-up call when Veronica left for a few days. For her part, Veronica is being supportive, but no longer appeasing.

Veronica hasn't given up trying hard to love her husband Vince, although she still finds him moody and negative some of the time. She is trying to make time for them to have a coffee and talk so that he can unload his day and relax.

Vince is a contractor working in construction, and finds his work interesting, but challenging. His sub-trades aren't dependable, and he gets pressure from his clients; he feels caught in the middle.

Veronica listens to Vince during T-Times (next chapter) and he unwinds. She is then able to challenge him to manage his moods better so that the children won't become upset with his behaviour. Because he has talked and unwound, Vince is more open to feedback and learns to cope with his frustrations in more constructive ways.

TIP: **Love challenges us to be the best we can be.**

"Let's review the Tips..."

- Give freely.
- Listen without giving away your power.
X - Your frame of reference can be a trap.
- Blaming blinds a person to his own faults.
- Unconditional lovers do not keep score.
- Kindness begets kindness.
X - Love with your willpower.
- Love challenges us to be the best we can be.

CHAPTER FOUR

T-Time

(Daily Talk-Time or Tea-Time)

At this precise moment, can you accurately guess what sort of day your spouse is having and how he/she is feeling? If you can answer "Yes", it probably means that you are making time each day to visit with one another in a feeling-focused conversation. If you can't, you may want to consider a "Daily T-Time."

The Daily T-Time has four steps:

1. Schedule the time.

2. Start with the mood of the moment.

3. Discuss what your day **did to you**.

4. Conduct marital business.

What follows is an outline for a **Daily T-Time**. This approach has helped many couples to effectively connect with each other through daily, meaningful conversation. Feel free to try it out or change it to fit your needs.

1. **Schedule the T-Time:** It may seem artificial to actually nail down a time to visit. However, if this step isn't taken, there's a good chance the day will pass with no opportunity for conversation. You don't need to select a specific time or place. It is more effective to be approximate (e.g. sometime between eight and ten at night). It is important, however, to find a time that's mutually convenient. Too early or too late doesn't usually work. It's fine for one partner to take the responsibility to initiate the conversations. This will work well as long as the other partner agrees with the arrangement.

2. **Start with the mood of the moment:** Either person can tentatively say what he or she thinks the other is feeling at that moment; for example: "Are you worried about something?" or "You seem tired." It's important not to ask, "How are you feeling?" or "What's wrong

with you?" Both of these well-intentioned inquiries can quickly lead to a dead end with an "I don't know" response. Also, to say "You're crabby tonight!" may backfire, as "crabby" is more a judgment call than a feeling. It's important, as well, to keep in mind that few people like to be told how they are feeling. They like to be asked, and to have the option of answering "Yes" or "No." It's also helpful to watch for non-verbal cues about how the other is feeling (i.e. expression, voice tone, and behaviour).

3. **Briefly discuss the moods of the day (five to ten minutes):** Talking about what you did that day may or may not interest your spouse. On the other hand, if you talk a little about **what your day did to you**, there's usually a better payoff, for two reasons. First of all, some of the tension created during the day is released by sharing it. Secondly, it allows you to connect with your mate because you are talking about some part of yourself. It's not the day's events or what we did or didn't do that matters. **What matters is how we felt about our day.**

Sometimes it's hard to recall various aspects of our day. It can be helpful, therefore, to make a mental note of four events during the day that can be brought up later in the T-Time (See *John and Joan* below). Three of the recollections can be distressful or neutral, but the fourth should always be positive. Always try to end the conversation with the positive or upbeat memory from the day.

4. **Do "Business":** At this stage of the T-Time, it's appropriate to move on to deal with issues of mutual importance. Possible topics could include finances, socializing, parenting challenges, or any other topics of joint concern. Consulting on a variety of topics can enrich a relationship. Where there is a difference of opinion (as there frequently will be), it's advisable to work towards a collaborative decision. Such teamwork also enriches a relationship; even if there's an agreement to disagree, the process will have been useful.

JOHN AND JOAN

After a tumultuous courtship, this couple have married and are moving ahead with their life together. John is committed to opening up more with Joan, and is overcoming his fears about doing so. He has a better understanding about commitment and what it takes to nourish their life together.

Four Events Noted

John and Joan have been working on their T-Times. John is reserved, and finds that he often doesn't have a lot to say about his day. Joan, on the other hand, is quite spontaneous with her thoughts, and will chat about various aspects of her day.

There are times when John says his piece in a moment or two, and Joan takes over and fills the rest of the time. Both are frustrated, as it seems that the talks are lopsided.

WHAT *is happening here?*

This couple is committed to doing T-Times, but John finds it harder to participate as openly as Joan.

TEAM TOOLS

Recalling and sharing four events or incidents from the day (and the associated feelings) can focus the T-Time and add structure to John and Joan's conversation. Each of them can make a mental or written note of occurrences that touched them in some way. It can be useful to make the fourth event a positive or funny experience.

It's important that John and Joan take turns sharing their recollections of the day so that one doesn't overwhelm the other; similar to a slow tennis game, with each taking turns to casually lob an aspect of their day.

Improving their T-Time:

John is now making mental notes during the day of things to mention to Joan. Sometimes he writes these ideas down so that he won't forget. Joan is also "flagging" some events from her day, even though she will have no trouble bringing things up during their talks.

✕ *During their T-Time whoever starts off then pauses so that the other can share his or her first event and associated feelings. John and Joan then go back and forth with their recollections, and invariably, other matters come up, and the talks flow much better. They both usually have a funny or absurd story to tell as well, and they end their talks with this sort of sharing.*

TIP: Give structure to your talks.

Nothing to Say Today

John has four events from the day but doesn't think that they had much impact upon him. He thinks he will mention them in passing and that will be it.

Joan asks a question about the third item John shares, to which he responds, and much to his surprise, a number of issues begin to surface that he didn't realize were bothering him. John tells Joan that he's surprised, as he thought he didn't have much to say. But as the talk gets rolling, it becomes apparent that more is going on than he realized.

WHAT is happening here?

John and Joan are doing well with their talks and find that sharing four aspects of their day has helped a lot. John shares with Joan how much he enjoyed a conversation with an electrical contractor, and he realizes, suddenly, that he misses the hands-on work he used to do at the beginning of his engineering career.

Joan and John are learning that their talks are like a treasure hunt with issues popping up out of the blue.

TEAM TOOLS

Sometimes when it seems like there isn't a lot to say, the T-Time reveals hidden concerns and emotions.

TIP: **T-Times can be more enlightening than we anticipate.**

KIM AND KEN

This couple have come a long way in their communication. Although Ken is reserved by nature, he's been opening up a lot more, and has also learned that he needs to listen. Kim has always been more open, and is also learning the value of improved listening.

Business Time

Ken and Kim are experimenting with the daily talks. They usually have a cup of tea or go for a walk in the evening, and after checking out each other's moods, they exchange some feelings around the events of the day.

There are decisions to make about the budget and an upcoming holiday, as well as concerns over their son's school performance. They discuss these issues last, and find that this aspect of their talk goes better than it used to. In the past, they would often argue over such topics.

WHAT is happening here?

This couple used to have difficulty making decisions together. Now they are more relaxed when they do business. By checking out each other's current moods and discussing some of the emotions of the day, they are easing their tensions and preparing themselves for further interaction.

TEAM TOOLS

Relationship business or sharing of information works best after personal exchanges about current moods and feelings from the day.

TIP: **Check out each other's moods before doing "business."**

MARK AND MOLLY

Introduction: Mark and Molly are a typical busy couple with a young family. Like some of the couples you met earlier, they spend little time conversing. They are similar to Ken and Kim in that Mark is reserved and doesn't see the need for much talk when he arrives home, and Molly is like Kim in that she wants more interaction.

Awkward At First

Mark and Molly know that they aren't talking enough with each other. They spend their days at the office and their evenings chauffeuring the children to their activities. Before they know it, it's time to fall into bed. Little time is left for the two of them to connect with each other.

Molly attends a preschool meeting and hears a talk about marriage, in which daily talks are proposed. She likes the idea, and takes it home to Mark. He tentatively agrees to give it a try. The next evening, Molly asks Mark if he's ready for their "daily talk" and he becomes anxious and draws a blank. He feels pressured, and the whole exercise seems artificial and awkward.

WHAT *is happening here?*

Mark and Molly are committed to improving their marriage. The idea of making some time to talk with each other on a regular basis makes sense, and they are willing to give it a try.

Mark is reticent by nature, and soon realizes that he's stressed about the idea of having to come up with daily topics of conversation. When Molly approaches him to have their talk, it sounds to him like a request to have a "summit conference," and it makes him even more nervous!

TEAM TOOLS

Daily talks, like any new behaviour, can seem artificial or awkward at first, but with some practice, this discomfort will often pass.

Making the time to talk:

Mark has been making time to have a visit with Molly most evenings. Some nights they are too busy or tired to do anything and they don't chat, but on several nights, they have made the time. Mark tells Molly that he has become more at ease with the talks. The initial discomfort has passed and he is rather enjoying the visits. Things seem warmer between the two of them.

TIP: Awkwardness or feelings of artificiality will pass.

It Doesn't Come Naturally

Mark and Molly are willing to make more time for each other and Molly has agreed to be the initiator. She likes to discuss her day, but is tired of trying to get the ball rolling, as Mark sometimes doesn't seem interested. Molly asks Mark if he's ready for their daily Talk-Time and he looks uncomfortable and says that he finds the daily talk format "too formal".

WHAT is happening here?

This couple have talked about the value of regular conversations and both have agreed that it's worth trying. When Molly brings up "Daily TalkTime", Mark finds the formality difficult, and often doesn't engage. He has been opening up more and is finding it less awkward, but the request from Molly still sounds like some "technique," and it makes him uncomfortable.

TEAM TOOLS

Daily talks or T-Times can occur in a low-key manner. Combining daily conversations with informal routines can make the talks seem more "natural" and less threatening. The important element is to find time to be alone together. As mentioned previously, it is not unusual for one spouse to be the initiator and this shouldn't be a concern, as long as the other mate generally agrees to participate in the T-Time.

Molly is sensitive to Mark's uneasiness, and decides to combine their talk with an evening tea break. This approach turns out to be much more relaxing for Mark, and he finds himself opening up more than he expected.

Talking over a cup of tea:

Molly asks Mark when he might like to take a tea break during the evening. Mark is working on the computer and agrees to break around eight-thirty. While drinking their tea, they chat about their day.

TIP: Just act naturally.

Think Out Loud

Mark and Molly are having a cup of tea and some conversation. Molly asks a few questions, and Mark doesn't have much to say. He likes the tea and talk, but sometimes doesn't know what to say. He thinks he has to mull an idea over and say something "significant." This thinking takes time, which results in long periods of silence.

WHAT is happening here?

When a person is not accustomed to participating in regular T-Times, it can be difficult to know what to say. Mark can see the value in the chats, but isn't sure what to talk about and how. He isn't spontaneous by nature and tends to do a lot of thinking before speaking.

TEAM TOOLS

Often, one spouse will be more spontaneous and speak freely. Her mate may not be so talented, and may find free-flowing conversation difficult. However, he may be a fluent thinker.

The conversation will move along well if the quieter spouse simply "thinks out loud." His mate will be pleased to hear whatever the thoughts are, as anything is better than frequent silences. If a disagreement should arise, they can work at resolving it openly instead of one of them withdrawing.

Improving their T-Time:

Molly and Mark are again having a cup of tea and doing their T-Time. Molly has just shared some of her day and talked about some difficulties she had with a workmate. Mark isn't sure how to help, and decides to say this out loud. He tells Molly that he senses her frustration and goes on to mention some other ideas that have just popped into his mind as he's speaking. Molly is surprised and pleased to hear Mark say so much all at once, particularly as she hasn't heard some of these ideas before.

TIP: Thinking out loud works!

Mood of the Moment

Mark and Molly are sharing their day. Mark jumps into some ideas about re-negotiating their mortgage. Molly seems distracted and even disinterested. Mark decides not to push his ideas and becomes silent.

Molly speaks up with some information about their kids. Mark is frustrated that Molly has changed the subject. He's worried about the mortgage and she hasn't noticed.

WHAT is happening here?

Jumping into business topics without first checking to see how the other person is feeling may lead to problems. It's good to start off a daily talk with some conversation about how each person is feeling in that present moment.

Mark and Molly have become good at making time most days to have tea together. They are aware of the suggested outline but haven't followed it that closely.

The "Daily T-Time" outline starts off with scheduling the talk. This couple prefer an informal tea time, and it's usually initiated by Molly. The second suggestion is that they check out each other's current feelings or "mood of the moment." Mark starts off with some thoughts about their mortgage, and doesn't first check out how Molly is feeling.

TEAM TOOLS

Ignored feelings can undermine an otherwise pleasant and productive discussion. Mark can ask Molly how her day is going or guess her mood from what he observes. This opening will allow Mark to discover that Molly is preoccupied and not ready for a discussion about mortgages.

Improving their T-Time:

Mark: *"Busy day?"*

Molly: *"A tiring one. I picked up Terri's dance schedule today and it's more complicated than I thought."*

Mark: *"Are you overwhelmed with the frequency?"*

Molly: *"Yes, and I'm concerned."*

Mark: *"Well I'm fine, a little bushed, but mostly worried about the mortgage renewal options."*

Molly: *"After we talk a little more about our day, why don't you tell me more about your concerns?"*

Mark: *"OK."*

TIP: Focus on feelings.

Don't Ask "How Are You Feeling?"

Molly: *"So, how are you feeling today?"*

Mark: *(pause)* *"I don't know."*

Molly: *"How can you not know how you are feeling?"*

Mark: *"I just don't. I never think about it."*

Molly: *"That's ridiculous."*

WHAT is happening here?

Molly has good intentions when she initiates their T-Time. She knows it's useful to focus upon feelings. Her husband Mark, however, isn't that tuned into emotions, and draws a blank. Molly, in turn, becomes frustrated.

TEAM TOOLS

Asking how someone is feeling may not be helpful, as the other person may legitimately not know! It's more helpful to guess a feeling. This can accomplish two things. It avoids conflict, as most people don't like to be told "how" they are feeling, but would rather be asked. Secondly, it helps a person to focus on his or her mood.

Instead of asking Mark what he's feeling, Molly can make a guess. This will allow Mark to become more self-aware. Molly's act of trying to listen to Mark will help him to hear himself as well. Molly doesn't have to guess correctly. Making any guess helps open up the conversation.

Your Turn...

(Cover the section below and write on a note pad how you might resolve this issue.)

Molly: *"Are you feeling tired?"*
Mark: *"Yeah, a little. Mostly, I'm frustrated with a situation at work."*
Molly: *"Is it that new project?*
Mark: *"No, it has to do with a shipment being delayed. We were supposed to get the new hardware today for the current job. It got stuck at the border."*
Molly: *"It's upsetting when this happens?"*
Mark: *"I'll say. Irritating as well. They promised a good delivery date and no problems with customs."*

TIP: Guess your spouse's feelings.

STAN AND SUSAN

This couple have come a long way since their short separation. Susan has adjusted her openness with Stan by trying not to overwhelm him with her ideas, and he has been speaking up more than he ever has in the past. Stan and Susan are treating each other with more kindness and are no longer playing the blame game.

Lots to Say Today

Stan has a busy and chaotic day and he's looking forward to spending some time chatting with Susan. They finish their dinner and while their children are doing homework, they head out for a short walk. Stan asks Susan how she's doing and she speaks briefly. Then Stan launches into his day. In a few moments, he finishes, and is feeling better, which surprises him. He thought he would have a lot more to say, but is finished sooner than he thought, and he feels great.

WHAT is happening here?

T-Times can be surprising. Stan had a challenging day and thinks he will have a lot to share during the visit with Susan. He shares a little, and perhaps because he's getting better at mentioning his feelings about the day, he's finished before he knows it. Susan and Stan then move on to discuss some family business.

TEAM TOOLS

Sometimes when it seems like there's a lot to say, the T-Time is over sooner than expected. This is more likely to happen if the listening is improving and feelings are being acknowledged as part of the conversation.

TIP: T-Times can be surprising.

VINCE AND VERONICA

Vince got a huge wake-up call when Veronica surprised him with a short separation. He told her that he didn't want to lose their marriage and that he was open to change. Veronica realized that she had been too passive and fearful to interact openly with Vince. She is now committed to doing things differently.

What Did Your Day Do to You?

Vince has been sharing more but doesn't like the idea of talking about his day during a T-Time. He believes that the best way to manage work stress is to leave it at work.

Vince mentions that his father worked in a mill when he was a kid and he came home and complained repeatedly about work issues. His father would do the complaining at the dinner table, and Vince made himself a promise that he wouldn't inflict such grumbling on his own family.

WHAT *is happening here*?

Vince is sincere in his attempt not to bring his work home. Unfortunately, he doesn't succeed as much as he thinks he does. He avoids talking about work, but is readily angry over small things with his children. He doesn't realize that his irritability and temperamental outbursts are related to the work stress he's ignoring.

TEAM TOOLS

Talking about what you did during the day is less effective than focusing upon "what the day did to you."

There are two suggestions for Vince. The first is to challenge his belief that he's leaving his work at work. He can try an experiment. He can talk a little about his day when he and Veronica have a cup of tea in the evening. Instead of talking or complaining about his day like his father did in the past, he can talk about how he "felt" about his day, i.e. what his day did to him in terms of his feelings. Was he happy or sad, frustrated or excited?

The second suggestion is not to use the dinner hour for this type of discussion. This is family time when the kids should be able to talk about their day with the parents listening and responding. If there are no kids, it can be a time for general information sharing and lighter discussion.

Improving their T-Time:

Veronica: *"How was your day?"*
Vince: *"Pretty good, considering."*
Veronica: *"Considering?"*
Vince: *"The new regulations came down today and they are ridiculous!"*
Veronica: *"You don't sound very happy."*
Vince: *"I'm furious! The regulators are so out of touch with reality.*
They don't ask our opinions, and then they dump this nonsense on us."
Veronica: *"Must seem insulting to all of you."*
Vince: *"Is it ever."*

TIP: **What your day did to YOU, in terms of feelings, is the focus!**

Build'n' Blow

Veronica asks Vince to mow the lawn. He is annoyed by the request and finds himself blowing up. In the back of his mind he's a little surprised at his upset, as the request from Veronica isn't that big of a deal. He complains about being overworked and withdraws.

WHAT is happening here?

When Vince blows up at Veronica, he surprises her and himself. Veronica mistakenly begins to "do business" with Vince without first taking a few moments to check out how he's doing. Often, she does take time to talk with him about "how his day felt," and yet he still seems to erupt with emotion.

TEAM TOOLS

Daily talks, though well intentioned, can be emotionally superficial, which leads to a build-up of tension. Veronica and Vince now talk most days, although Vince still blows up. This probably means that in addition to being tired, Vince isn't talking enough about his feelings during their talks. When emotions aren't shared regularly and thoroughly, they seem to build up, and a small issue can trigger an inappropriately large reaction.

Veronica and Vince pick up where they left off:

Veronica tells Vince that she isn't intending to annoy him by asking him to mow the lawn. She adds that her timing may be a little off. Vince admits that he's surprised by the intensity of his reaction. He is tired, but his level of upset indicates that there's something more going on. He then recalls a few smaller issues that are bothering him.

Veronica remembers discussing these issues, and realizes that their talk was superficial and analytical. She didn't realize that Vince felt so strongly about the topics he raised.

TIP: Unshared feelings can accumulate.

Walk 'n' Talk

Veronica and Vince have been doing T-Times regularly and are building some momentum. If a day passes when they aren't able to talk over a cup of tea they miss the connection, and try harder the next day to make sure they get together.

Veronica enjoys walking with her girlfriend, and asks Vince if he'd like to go for a walk with her instead of having tea. Vince is warming to the T-Times, but isn't yet overly enthused about doing them each day. He isn't a big walker, and turns down the invitation.

WHAT is happening here?

Veronica appreciates the effort Vince has made to join her for regular T-Times, but knows it's hard for him. She enjoys walking and is keen to get Vince out for some fresh air and exercise as well. Veronica and her girlfriend find it easy to talk while walking, and in the back of her mind, she thinks it might be the same for her and Vince. Veronica is disappointed, but not surprised that Vince turns down her invitation to walk and talk.

TEAM TOOLS

Going for a walk while doing T-Times can work well. Vince can stretch out of his comfort zone a bit to do something that makes his wife happy. The important thing is that they spend some time together.

Improving their T-Time:

After Vince had turned down Veronica's invitation to walk with her, he noticed her disappointment. The following evening, he tells Veronica that he'd like to go for a walk with her.

Vince feels closer to Veronica because of the talks they've been having, and so it's not a big stretch for him to walk with her. He finds the experience less intense than sitting across from Veronica while having tea, and he ends up talking more comfortably for a longer period of time.

TIP: Try walking for a low-key T-Time.

"Let's review the Tips..."

• Give structure to your talks.

• T-Times can be more enlightening than we anticipate.

• Check out each other's moods before doing "business."

• Awkwardness or feelings of artificiality will pass.

• Just act naturally.

• Thinking out loud works.

• Focus on feelings.

• Guess your spouse's feelings.

• T-Times can be surprising.

• What your day did to YOU, in terms of feelings, is the focus!!

• Unshared feelings can accumulate.

• Try walking for a low-key T-Time.

CHAPTER FIVE

Listening Basics

It might be helpful to review some fundamental listening guidelines.

Generally speaking, we are not taught in school how to listen well, and may be unaware of the steps that can really make a difference in the way we interact with each other.

I've outlined a few effective techniques that will help bring harmony to your interactions with loved ones. These are common sense ideas, which can often be forgotten when trying to communicate with others.

Eye Contact: Look into the eyes of the other person at least some of the time when conversing.

Empty Your Head: Focus on the person who is speaking without thinking about your response.

No Interruptions: Allow the speaker to finish his thought without cutting in.

Responding: Give feedback to the speaker as to what you are hearing.

Repeated Message: A speaker will repeat herself if she thinks she hasn't been heard the first time.

Non-Responsive Listener: Just because a listener doesn't offer a response, it doesn't mean he hasn't heard you.

Focus on a Feeling: Many messages have both thought and feeling components. Acknowledging the feeling is a good first step. And it is a step worth repeating frequently thereafter.

Listen Always: It is important to not only listen when another person talks to you, but also to observe your listener when you are speaking. Try to see the impact of the message you are sharing.

Listening Tips

1. **Have an "Attitude of Other-Centeredness":** We have to abandon our own frame of reference or way of understanding a situation, and truly enter into that of the other person. It doesn't matter whether we understand why there is a problem, or even what the difficulty might be. Rather, we can compassionately hear and accept the upset, worry, or frustration of the person delivering the message. The problem solving comes later. To be compassionate is to **feel another person's pain, or to walk a while in her shoes.**

2. **Be Observant:** We listen with our eyes, watching for clues as to what the other person may be feeling inside; posture, movement, facial expression, paleness or redness of the skin and moistness of the eyes are all significant. The tone of voice is also an indication that there might be more going on than just the obvious.

3. **Be Warm/Hospitable:** When a friend visits our home, we usually greet him warmly and treat him with kindness. During the visit, we focus on our friend in an expression of support or affection. Effective listeners do the same. We treat the speaker as someone who has come for a visit. With company in our home, we don't usually wander off to take care of solitary activities. It is easy for us as listeners, however, to wander off in our minds while the other person is talking. The speaker can tell that we've tuned out and that our coolness has replaced the warmth.

4. **Concentrate:** The challenge for us as listeners is to free our minds of everything, so as to be **empty.** In this way, we are more likely to have room for the story of the other person. Also, without our own agenda to distract us, we can better focus on what the speaker is saying.

5. **Accept:** Often when we listen, we fall into the trap of agreement, disagreement, or advice giving, rather than accepting what is being described or felt. The talker simply wants to be heard and understood without any value judgment placed upon their experience.

   To agree too enthusiastically with the speaker who is complaining about his difficulties with another person may cause the speaker to defend the one who is the source of his upset. In agreeing, we also make the problem seem worse than it is.

To disagree can also create difficulties. Trying to help a person who is complaining to see the other side of the problem is certainly important. However, if it happens too soon, he will become upset with us because it seems like we are taking sides with the one who is the source of the problem.

To give advice, particularly early in the conversation, may prove futile. We would be wise to invite the speaker to suggest some solutions of her own. This is more helpful than simply rushing to the rescue with our own ideas.

Often, advice is offered because we're uncomfortable with the message we hear, and we want to fix things quickly. The unintentional message behind a lot of advice-giving is that the solution is obvious and the upset person must be "stupid" not to have figured it out earlier.

6. **Be Responsive:** It's important for us to prove that we are really trying to hear the other person. There are non-verbal ways of showing attention, such as eye contact (which is also an indicator of concentration). Other non-verbal means of responding include posture, expression, nods of the head, and even little sounds of affirmation.

A common, yet often unhelpful listener response is "I understand how you feel." It's good that the listener is voicing a response to the speaker; however, this one is too general. The speaker may say to himself "No you don't. You aren't me; how could you really know my feelings?" Generally, when we give feedback, we need to indicate by our words and actions that we are **hearing**.

7. **Use Willpower:** In recent years within popular psychology, there has been a great deal of emphasis on the importance of feelings. Some people have come to believe that if a certain feeling occurs, it should be taken seriously; however, there is something equally important as one's feelings. That something is the **relationship** we have with another person.

If a speaker is upset and needs to talk and we are tired, we may say that we are too tired to be supportive (believing our own emotion to be important). True, there may be times when the talk will have to be delayed. However, most of the time, we can make a willful decision to listen in spite of our current mood. Or, the speaker can make a willful decision to share her upset later, or temporarily put it aside so as to focus upon the listener's fatigue. Any parent will tell you that there's a part of him or her that is stronger than how he or she feels. This under utilized aspect of all of us is called **willpower**. (Chapter 3 – Unconditional Love)

As mentioned above, it is important to always listen whether we are speaking or not. If we are listening while we are talking, we can occasionally invite the listener to share his reactions; i.e. "Are you finding it hard to listen to me talk about these matters? Would you like to stop now?" Willpower can be helpful in switching gears from speaker to listener, rather than becoming offended at not being heard properly.

8. **Forgive:** Committed couples have a bond of unconditional love between them. To keep this bond healthy, they will have to forgive each other frequently. There can be misunderstandings within relationships, which lead to hurt feelings. Once these feelings are aired and accepted, it's necessary to forgive so as to move ahead. Without the forgiveness, the hurt feelings will return with a vengeance. To forgive doesn't mean that whatever happened was really fine; it wasn't. However, if there's no forgiveness, the partners become blind and deaf to their own fault in the problem situation.

Here is a step-by-step outline for improving listening:

Step 1: Be quiet.

Step 2: Perceive what the other person is saying verbally (note the tone) and with their body (posture and gestures).

Step 3: Interpret the message (focus first on the feelings of the speaker).

Step 4: Check out your interpretation by guessing the feeling you are sensing.

Step 5: Hear the response.

Step 6: If your guess is not correct, he should then be able to tell you what he is feeling.

Step 7: If your guess is correct, ask if he wants to discuss the feeling or situation.

Step 8: Give feedback on ideas he shared.

Step 9: Observe the reaction to your feedback, and focus, once again, on any emotion.

Step 10: Check out your interpretation.

Step 11: Discuss ideas.

Scenario A

Speaker: (said with authority and tone) "Don't put those branches in a bag. They need to be tied with string!"

Listener: (reacting to the bossy tone of the other) "They're fine in a bag."

Speaker: "No they're not; the bag rips. It's better to tie them."

Listener: (angry) "Why don't you just do it yourself?"

Here the speaker expresses her opinion in an authoritative way. The listener doesn't like to be told what to do and reacts poorly to the "order." The speaker ignores the listener and repeats her idea; the listener becomes angry and withdraws.

Scenario B (improved)

Speaker: (said with authority) "Don't put those branches in a bag. They need to be tied with a string!"

Listener: (hearing the tone but not reacting) "Does it bother you that I'm bagging the branches?"

Speaker: "No, I just think it works better tying them."

Listener: "To me, you sounded angry."

Speaker: "I'm feeling tired this morning. I'm not angry. I've bagged branches before, and the bags rip easily."

Scenario C (also improved)

Speaker: "Don't put those branches in a bag. They need to be tied with a string!"

Listener: "They're fine in a bag."

Speaker: "I don't mean to be a pain. I just think that it works better if they're tied. The bag rips easily."

Listener: "Well I don't disagree. I asked Danielle (their daughter) to tie them, and she said she didn't know how to do it."

Speaker: "Really? She and I tied the branches last spring. Perhaps we should have another branch tying session. She'll be thrilled at that idea, I'm sure."

CHAPTER SIX

To Listen Is To Love

Listening is an art form.

• Do I listen only to the words of a speaker and miss the feelings?	Y	N
• Do my feelings get in the way when I'm listening to others?	Y	N
• Do I have trouble putting myself in other people's shoes?	Y	N
• Do I ignore people's eyes and posture when they talk to me?	Y	N
• Do I find my mind wandering when I am listening?	Y	N
• Do I agree or disagree rather than simply accept what I hear?	Y	N
• Do I have trouble listening if I do not understand why the speaker is upset?	Y	N
• Do I give advice right away?	Y	N

If you answered YES to any two of these questions, your listening skills may need to be tuned up.

Many people see themselves as "good communicators" just because they are adept at expressing themselves. Little do they know that listening is the key skill in communication, and they are probably not as competent at it as they think. Effective listening and humility go hand in hand. It takes skill, practice, and a keen awareness of the difficulties involved in order to improve in this area.

One way to discover if you are a good listener is to ask a loved one: "Please be open with me; do I give you and others the impression that I'm not listening sometimes?" Hopefully, your family member or friend will feel comfortable pointing out how you come across. "Well, sometimes you seem distracted or annoyed when I try to talk to you."

When we listen well, we help to **liberate** the speaker from upset and confusion. At times, a person can be so caught up within his own experience that he's unsure of what he feels. An effective listener will facilitate self-understanding in the speaker. For instance, the speaker's tone may have an edge to it. So instead of saying, "Don't use that tone with me," the listener might say, "Are you feeling tired?" or "You sound upset with me."

There are many obstacles to effective listening. Here are two examples:

a. Many people are "reactive" listeners. They respond to what is said according to their own feelings and give little thought to what might be happening inside the other person. They may say something like, "I hate it when you talk to me like that."

b. At the other end of the scale, some of us, because of childhood experience, have learned to ignore our own reaction and to focus completely on the underlying message of the other person. We make excuses for them and may say to ourselves "He said that nasty thing because he's tired; he didn't really mean it." Nothing is said about the hurtful message or the underlying feeling, and the listener thinks it's not safe to say anything.

Either extreme style of listening isn't productive. In the first instance, we're completely caught up in what's happening to us. In the other, we forget ourselves and let the other person off the hook, even though he has shared a feeling in an inappropriate fashion. In both cases, our method of listening hasn't been effective or helpful, and the speaker will not **feel** well heard by us.

When I was a student learning about psychology, there was a lot of emphasis on sharing one's emotions. It was viewed as important, and the assumption seemed to be that if a person opened up and spoke her truth, i.e. her feelings of the moment, the other would magically listen and respond supportively.

I recall one evening being frustrated with my wife, and I told her so. She looked at me and responded differently than I expected. Instead of acknowledging my emotion and then enquiring as to why I was frustrated, she paused, and then told me that she was frustrated too. I was surprised, as I was so caught up in my own experience that it hadn't occurred to me that she was also feeling upset. When I told her, "I was frustrated first," she replied, "So?" We both laughed.

In that moment we learned that regardless of our individual feelings about some issue, someone had to listen first and then talk afterwards. I made up a little adage for myself at that time, which I've tried to remember over the years: "Listen first and frequently thereafter."

Intent vs. Impact

Every message has both an "**intent**" and an "**impact**." A common scenario illustrates this point:

A wife expresses upset feelings about a lazy co-worker. The husband gives advice to his wife about how to handle the problem. The wife then becomes even more upset, and directs her anger towards her husband for giving unsolicited advice.

The husband is now offended that his advice hasn't been well received, and takes it as a personal rejection. The wife is equally offended that her husband has ignored or discounted the strong feelings she was experiencing.

They start to argue. She says that he's ignoring her upset. He says he's not ignoring anything; he's simply trying to be helpful. She counters by saying that he isn't helping at all.

In reality, they are both right.

His **intent** was to offer help, but the **impact** on her was quite different. When she spoke about the impact, she ignored his intent, and vice versa. Every exchange has these two components. It's necessary to acknowledge the validity of both the intent and impact. An example of how to do this is:

Him: "You seem annoyed with me for giving you advice right now."

Her: "I am. You're always giving me advice instead of just listening to me. I realize that you're concerned about me and my problem. However, I don't want your advice right now; I just want you to hear my frustration. We can talk about what to do about it later."

You probably **hear** other people when they talk to you. But to really **listen** is to **acknowledge** and **accept** both the feeling and the message. To **react** is to listen and respond to one's own feelings.

BETH AND BOB

Beth and Bob have their differences and are trying to adjust to each other's priorities. Bob expresses his feelings freely, while Beth tends to withdraw for fear of upsetting others.

Rejection

Beth suffers from depression. She keeps most of her thoughts to herself, particularly those that might upset her family and friends.

Bob is more vocal and thinks out loud. He's concerned about Beth and has asked her to speak up more. He wants her to say what's on her mind, even if it may bother him to hear it. He reassures her that he "can handle it" and he does... for a time!

But the day arrives when Bob reacts angrily to something that Beth has shared. He yells, withdraws into himself, and pouts. Beth now feels guilty for speaking up and begins to reconsider her plan to be more open. She also withdraws and becomes more guarded in what she says.

WHAT is *happening here?*

Bob and Beth's plan has been working well. It's just a matter of time, however, before Beth says something that irritates Bob. On this occasion he's tired, and instead of listening in a supportive fashion, he reacts to her comments with anger.

Bob has encouraged Beth to be open, but he seems to punish her for doing so. This is confusing for Beth. She experiences rejection and guilt, and returns to being guarded.

TEAM TOOLS

Beth has worked hard at opening up more and overcoming a long-standing cautiousness. She used to take on too much responsibility for the feelings of those around her, but she's now allowing Bob and her children their emotions without taking ownership of them. However, there are times when her feelings may get in the way of this new approach and cause her to slip back into the old pattern.

Beth can let Bob have his feelings even though she's uncomfortable with the anger, and realize that the feelings don't detract from his love for her. Instead of ignoring him, Beth can ask Bob if he's bothered by her request and if he wants to talk. She can still allow him the option of not talking at this time.

Listening with acceptance:

Beth tells Bob about a job in the garden that needs doing and he becomes upset. He accuses her of "never letting up with the chores," and retreats to his favourite chair in the living room.

Instead of apologizing and backing down from her request, Beth approaches Bob. She asks him if he's upset with her, and if so, whether he wants to talk. He denies that he's upset. She tells him that if he changes his mind, she's willing to talk. Beth then returns to what she was doing.

TIP: *Accept the feelings of another person.*

It's Got to be Me

Bob and Beth are taking a walk and doing their T-Time.

Beth: *(sensing that Bob is feeling down because he's so quiet)* "Did you hear that joke Harry told the group the other night?"
Bob: *"Nope."* (silence)
Beth: *"Have I done something wrong?"*
Bob: *"Nope."* (more silence)

WHAT is happening here?

Walking together can be a great time to have a talk. Beth is perceptive and can sense that Bob is upset.

Beth, as we know, finds Bob's moods uncomfortable. When someone she loves is upset, Beth thinks it must be her fault. This way of thinking has followed her from childhood when she was often blamed for things, even when it wasn't her fault.

Instead of tuning into Bob's feeling, Beth finds it scary and tunes into her own fear. Bob doesn't start to talk and his mood continues to be ignored.

TEAM TOOLS

Picking up on another person's feeling is one thing; listening well is another. If the listener is uncomfortable with what she thinks she hears, she may inappropriately find some way to distract the speaker.

Beth is perceptive and can focus on the mood that Bob seems to be in during their walk. The resulting conversation can help both parties feel more at ease.

Your Turn...

(Cover the section below and write on a note pad how you might resolve this issue.)

Learning to listen:

Beth: *(sensing that Bob is feeling down because he's so quiet)* "Did you hear that joke Harry told the group the other night?"
Bob: *"Nope." (silence)*
Beth: *"You seem far away."*
Bob: *"Oh, I'm worried about Dad."*
Beth: *"Have you heard some news?"*
Bob: *"Mom called to say the test results were not good."*
Beth: *"Scary, isn't it?"*
Bob: *"It sure is." (tears)*
Beth: *(hugs Bob)*

TIP: **Acceptance leads to greater openness.**

GORD AND GINA

Gord and Gina are opposites: Gord shares his thoughts openly, and Gina tends to hold back. She's hesitant to bring up aspects of Gord's behaviour that bother her for fear he will dismiss her concerns.

Little Girl Listening

Gord and Gina are having a heated discussion about dealing with an unreliable repairman.

Gord: *(irritation in his tone)* "That plumber hasn't called."
Gina: *"Would you like me to call him?"*
Gord: *"I don't know what good that'll do."*
Gina: *"Why don't we go out and have a coffee?"*
Gord: *(increased agitation)* "I don't feel like going anywhere. I want this drainage problem fixed!"

WHAT is happening here?

When Gord becomes irritable or angry, Gina does her best to lie low or make things better for Gord. Gina is very uncomfortable with Gord's anger and will try to make it go away by appeasing or pleasing him. Sometimes this works, sometimes it doesn't. Most often things worsen, leaving Gina feeling frustrated, scared, and guilty.

When Gina was a young girl, there was a time when she would openly share her thoughts and feelings. However, she noticed that when she offered negative feedback about certain actions or comments that her parents made, she frequently got into trouble for doing so. She soon learned after a few of these incidents that it was better not to say anything.

It was difficult, however, for Gina, as a child, to reconcile her feelings; perhaps she subconsciously redefined what was happening. She was dependent and needed her father's love, so she couldn't do or say anything to jeopardize her relationship with her caregiver. Her father said things that hurt her and occasionally he even struck her. She couldn't speak up, as it made things worse.

Young Gina, therefore, took her upset feelings and turned inwards. Her dependency on her parents didn't allow her to hold them responsible, and so she took the blame upon herself. As an adult, Gina now takes the blame for her husband's moods.

Gina has now moved from appeasement to angry impatience.

Gord: *(irritation in his voice)* *"That plumber still hasn't called."*
Gina: *"He'll get to us; he's probably really busy."*
Gord: *"Just because he's busy, do we have to be forgotten?"*
Gina: *(frustration and anger in her tone)* *"There you go again, getting all bent out of shape for no big reason."*
Gord: *(increased agitation)* *"Whose side are you on anyway?"*
Gina: *(also angry)* *"You handle it next time if you're so smart."*

WHAT *is happening here?*

Gina is tired of trying to "fix things" for Gord. Over time, it has worn her down, and she's very tired and frustrated. Her old fears and worries have been overtaken by her new feelings of frustration and anger.

Gina has now decided to stand up for herself more. By reacting to Gord's anger with her own anger, Gina has gone from one extreme to the other. In her attempt to change, Gina has gone from a passive to an aggressive style of communication.

Gina may be challenging Gord more, but because she still takes responsibility for his feelings and behaviour, she now feels guilty that he's angry or upset with her for her changed approach.

TEAM TOOLS

When an appeaser becomes tired of trying to make things better all the time, she can swing like a pendulum to the other extreme. Angry impatience with the feelings of another is no more productive than being too accommodating.

When Gord is angry, instead of appeasing or attacking, Gina can try to accept his mood and discuss it with him if he's open to doing so. If he isn't, they can leave it until later.

If Gina forgets to listen effectively and attacks Gord when he's angry, he has a choice as well. He can react in anger, as he usually does, or he can acknowledge and accept Gina's anger and discuss it with her. If he does this, he will soon learn that the feeling that's hiding behind her anger is discomfort with his upset.

When Gord acts in an irritable manner Gina can ask him if he's tired or frustrated. This approach isn't the old assumption-based "pleasing style" or the assumption-based "attack style." Instead of deciding what mood he's in and trying to change it, Gina can now ask Gord for his opinion. Together, they are then able to release the mood through discussion. This is what happens when a feeling is focused upon in a non-judgmental and non-controlling fashion.

Learning to listen:

Gord: *(irritation in his tone)* *"That plumber still hasn't shown up."*

Gina: *(acknowledging his feeling)* *"I'm annoyed too."*

Gord: *(trying to place blame)* *"He should be here on time, and you should have made that clear to him."*

Gina: *(acknowledging the feeling, refusing to get defensive)* *"We're both frustrated, but all we can do is give him another call."*

Gord: *(starting to calm down)* *"I just wish people would honour their commitments."*

Gina: *(a helpful suggestion)* *"Me too. Do you want to call him or should I?"*

TIP: **Checking out feelings first makes for better listening.**

Silent Listening

Gina and Gord are doing some chores and Gord expresses some frustration and anger with the mess left by the children. Gina can tell that Gord is angry, and asks him about it. Her enquiry seems to make Gord even angrier, and he snaps back, "Of course I'm angry, isn't that obvious?"

TEAM TOOLS

When another person is obviously angry or frustrated, acknowledging the anger may seem to intensify the upset. It may be prudent to remain silent until the intensity of the feelings subsides. Helping in a practical way may be the best response. Taking time to reflect on how to proceed as a listener can be helpful as well.

If the anger is acknowledged, as above, and the response is similar to that of Gord, Gina could simply say, "Would you like to talk about it?" or "I'm feeling uncomfortable."

Learning to listen:

Another occasion arises when Gord loudly expresses frustration at how slow the computer is operating. Gina has picked up on Gord's upset, but senses that "stating the obvious" might escalate things, even though she's trying to be understanding. In the past she would try to appease Gord's concern, but lately she's been listening openly.

Gina has been speaking up about her impressions, but on this occasion realizes that she can listen and remain silent. Mentally noting Gord's feeling and then doing something to ease his tensions works well for both of them. This is not an appeasement as later on, when things settle down, they will speak more openly about the feelings that arose earlier.

TIP: Listening but not commenting is appropriate at times.

Little Boy Sad

Gord and Gina have taken their children on a long anticipated camping trip. They are now sitting around their campfire having a drink and a T-Time and are beginning to unwind. A few campsites over, they hear a small boy crying loudly. Gord looks at Gina and says, "What a racket! How are we supposed to relax and unwind with that kid bellowing? Where are his parents?"

WHAT is happening here?

Gord is tired from working all week and the long drive, and is triggered by the little boy who is upset.

> **TEAM TOOLS**
>
> Listening without reacting is a great challenge! Sitting around a campfire with a drink is a relaxing experience and sets the stage for some good listening.
>
> However, good intentions are often foiled by one's own tensions and fatigue. This chapter is entitled "To Listen is To Love" because effective listening requires willpower. Gord finds it hard to hear the anguish of the young boy, and reacts instead. Like most of us, Gord can work harder at listening, particularly when he's feeling tired himself.

Your Turn...

(Cover the section below and write on a note pad how you might re-solve this issue.)

A few campsites over, a small boy is crying loudly. Gord looks at Gina and says, "Someone sounds sad or tired." Gina nods. It occurs to Gord that he has just done something unique. Instead of getting annoyed with the unhappy little neighbour, he's read between the lines and picked up on his upset rather than focusing on the behaviour. He mentions to Gina that he's surprised because he would usually complain about the noise, with little thought given to the boy's feelings.

TIP: **Hear the feelings behind the words.**

HANNA AND HARVEY

Harvey is uncomfortable with confrontation. Hanna, who is more di-rect, is frustrated by Harvey's avoidance of discussing or confronting problems.

Look At Those Cows

Hanna and Harvey are discussing a promise Harvey made about drink-ing less and losing weight.

Hanna: *"It annoys me when you don't follow through on a promise."*
Harvey: *"What do you mean?"*
Hanna: *"You said you wouldn't have a drink for a week, and you ordered a beer with lunch."*
Harvey: *"I don't recall saying no drinks at all."*
Hanna: *"Yes you did!"*
Harvey: *"Look at those cows over there. You don't see that colour combination that often."*

WHAT *is happening here?*

This couple are having a chat while driving together through the countryside. Hanna raises a sensitive topic and Harvey begins to feel uncomfortable. As the discussion heats up, Harvey decides to change the subject. Hanna becomes very angry and stops talking.

Hanna is offended by a tendency she has observed in Harvey. He seems to change the subject a lot when she has a concern that's frustrating to her. In turn, Hanna misses or ignores Harvey's discomfort and doesn't ask him if there's a reason he changes the subject. Harvey doesn't like to argue, and changes the subject to avoid problems.

TEAM TOOLS

When a conversation seems threatening, it can be tempting for the person feeling upset to change the topic. However, changing the subject doesn't chase feelings away; sometimes it even amplifies them.

Hanna has criticized Harvey for not following through with what she thought was their plan about his drinking. Harvey doesn't like trouble, but doesn't need to let this sensitivity get in the way of his listening to Hanna's upset feelings and explaining his perspective. In this way, any misunderstandings can be cleared up.

Following are two other ways the above conversation could have unfolded:

Hanna: *"It annoys me when you don't follow through on a promise."*
Harvey: *"What do you mean?"*
Hanna: *"You said you wouldn't have a drink for a week, and you ordered a beer with lunch."*
Harvey: *"I don't recall saying no drinks at all."*
Hanna: *"Yes you did!"*
Harvey: *"Are you annoyed with me for having a beer?"*
Hanna: *"You said you wanted to lose some weight."*
Harvey: *"I do want to lose weight, and cutting back on the booze is a*

good plan. I don't want to stop living though. I think the odd drink should be fine. I'm sorry if I misled you."

Hanna: *"That sounds reasonable. We have to be careful though."*

Or

Hanna: *"It annoys me when you don't follow through on a promise."*

Harvey: *"What do you mean?"*

Hanna: *"You said you wouldn't have a drink for a week, and you ordered a beer with lunch."*

Harvey: *"I don't recall saying no drinks at all."*

Hanna: *"Yes you did!"*

Harvey: *"Look at those cows over there. You don't see that colour combination that often."*

Hanna: *"Does it make you uncomfortable when I bring up drinking?"*

Harvey: *"Well, I don't want to argue about it."*

Hanna: *"Neither do I. I'm just worried about you."*

TIP: Changing the subject may indicate underlying discomfort.

Did You Hear What I Meant to Say?

Harvey and his son, Sean, are having a discussion about a party Sean will be attending. Harvey is concerned about the remote location, but Sean interprets his father's concern as interference, and becomes annoyed.

An argument ensues with each of them forcefully restating his ideas, but neither of them getting anywhere.

Harvey now realizes that Sean is annoyed and tries to clarify his point, as he isn't intending to fluster his son. He's simply doing his fatherly advice thing and it blows up on him. Sean is convinced that his dad is trying to hassle him and he's not in the mood. The reality is that Sean is also a little tired from a late night.

As the discussion progresses, other topics are dragged in and it looks like things are about to deteriorate into a shouting match. Harvey calls a time-out (see Chapter 8) and they stop to cool down and ease tensions.

WHAT *is happening here?*

These two well-intentioned family members initially got into trouble because they had a common misunderstanding. Harvey offered advice, and Sean heard differently.

They are destined to argue because they are talking about two different realities. Harvey intends to be helpful, and yet his son hears a different message. The impact on Sean is more like an attack. They are getting nowhere.

TEAM TOOLS

It's tempting to try and clarify an issue when another person is upset by what we're saying. If we can just get across what we meant to say, the other person will feel better, but they seem to feel worse the more we say.

First of all, Harvey can acknowledge his son's irritation. (He had picked up on it, but didn't realize he needed to check it out.) If he asks his son if he's upset by the conversation, Sean can say he is. Once a feeling is acknowledged, further discussion is usually possible.

Harvey's mistake was jumping right into his clarification, and Sean rejects it, partly because his unacknowledged feeling gets in the way.

Sean assumes that his dad is hassling him, partly because of Harvey's tone. He doesn't ask his dad if he's annoyed or worried; he simply reacts due to his own upset.

This pair doesn't realize that there can be an unintentional discrepancy between what is said and what is heard. There can be the intent to be helpful, and the impact of being bossed around. There can be the intent of sharing a concern, and the impact of being talked down to.

Learning to listen:

Harvey: *"Have I irritated you by what I just said?"*
Sean: *"Yeah, you're always telling me what to do!"*
Harvey: *"I don't mean to sound bossy; I'm only trying to offer a little advice. I worry about you when you and your friends party out in the bush."*

Or:

Sean: *"Are you annoyed with me?"*
Harvey: *"No. Do I sound annoyed?"*
Sean: *"Yeah."*
Harvey: *"I'm not annoyed; I'm worried about you and the guys partying while camping."*
Sean: *"Well, thanks for caring. We'll take it easy."*

TIP: Listen first, clarify second, and then listen some more.

Tone Well Heard

It's getting close to dinner time and Harvey calls his daughter, Carrie. He shouts so that she will hear him since she's in her room with the door closed. Hanna, who is standing nearby, tells Harvey not to talk to their daughter "so sternly." Harvey denies that he has, saying that he has simply called Carrie for dinner. He becomes annoyed with Hanna for challenging him, yet again, on his parenting.

WHAT is happening here?

Harvey is surprised that Hanna thinks he's speaking "sternly" to their daughter, as this isn't his intention. He becomes annoyed with Hanna for accusing him of something he doesn't believe he's done. He doesn't think to ask Hanna if she's uncomfortable with the way he called Carrie.

TEAM TOOLS

It is helpful to acknowledge an emotion instead of reacting to an angry tone of voice. This can be a challenge, but is helpful for mutual understanding. When Hanna hears something in Harvey's tone, she can ask him if he's annoyed with Carrie, rather than criticizing him for his tone of voice. This approach allows Harvey to self-examine without feeling attacked.

Here's another way the above story could have unfolded:

Harvey calls his daughter, Carrie, for dinner. Hanna, who is standing nearby, asks him if he's annoyed with their daughter. He says that he isn't, and asks Hanna if it sounds like he is. She says that for her, it sounded like he was annoyed. He thinks for a moment and acknowledges that he's tired and perhaps he sounds stern when he is tired.

Carrie sticks her head out of her door and asks what her father wants. He tells her that it's time for dinner. Carrie asks him if he's annoyed with her. He laughs and says that he isn't. He says he's tired and that must be why he sounded upset. He then asks Carrie, jokingly, if her mother phoned her in her room. He finds the similarity of their response to him pleasantly unsettling.

Harvey will monitor his tone more carefully in the future.

TIP: Checking out a tone of voice is better than reacting to it.

Mr. Cranky

It's has been a long day. Harvey, Hanna and the family have just finished an eleven-hour road trip, and Harvey has done all the driving.

Harvey is sitting in the kitchen having a snack and reading the newspaper when his youngest daughter, Jane, comes in and asks him several rapid-fire questions. Harvey turns to her and tells her, with obvious irritation, to stop "nattering" at him. Immediately, Harvey notices the look on her face and can tell that he's hurt her.

Hanna is standing nearby. She tells Harvey not to speak to Jane in this way. Harvey immediately becomes upset with Hanna, and tells her to mind her own business. Jane leaves the room in tears.

WHAT is happening here?

Harvey is tired, and when interrupted, snaps at his daughter. He is about to apologize, but before he has a chance to do so, Hanna reprimands him.

TEAM TOOLS

It is very helpful to show that an underlying feeling lies beneath the words of one family member towards another. Harvey realizes that he has unintentionally hurt his daughter's feelings. Hanna can facilitate understanding for Jane by offering an example of good listening to her daughter. Such a gesture will be welcomed by Harvey, rather than be seen as a criticism of his behaviour.

Here's another way the above story could have unfolded:

Harvey is sitting in the kitchen having a snack when his youngest daughter, Jane, comes in and asks him several rapid-fire questions. Harvey turns to her and tells her, with obvious irritation, to stop "nattering" at him. Immediately, Harvey notices the look on her face and can tell that he's hurt her.

Hanna is standing nearby and she turns to their daughter and says, "I think that maybe Dad is tired after our long trip."

Harvey apologizes to Jane and confirms that indeed he is feeling very tired, but this fatigue is no excuse for "barking" at her. The look of hurt passes from her face almost immediately and Harvey invites Jane to repeat her questions.

Later, Harvey thanks Hanna for her supportive comment.

TIP: Good listening leads to good listening.

KEN AND KIM

Ken has been opening up more lately and really listening to Kim. She is becoming less reactive and is also starting to listen more to Ken.

It's All About Me

Ken and Kim have been talking regularly during their T-Time. However, from time to time, they run into trouble.

Ken: *"I think you should skip your plan to travel to the Island."*
Kim: *"Why would you say that?"*
Ken: *"I don't think the dollars are there right now."*
Kim: *"Right now? You never think the dollars are there!"*
Ken: *"Oh, forget it. Everything is an argument with you!"*

WHAT is happening here?

Many couples avoid regular talks, as they worry about just such a conversation. Kim and Ken have slipped into an argument. Their differences of opinion on money management, along with poor listening, have caused dissension.

Ken is very security-conscious and likes to have a nest egg in the bank. Money has been particularly tight lately due to some unforeseen expenses. He knows that Kim has a trip planned with a couple of girl friends, and he has been stewing about it for weeks, afraid to bring the topic up.

Ken broaches the subject and sure enough, Kim is defensive right away. Ken is already tense, and her response increases his tension. He forges ahead with his concern, Kim starts to "lose it," and Ken becomes even more tense. He drops the topic.

Kim is surprised when Ken brings up her trip to the Island. It annoys her that he suggests that she skip her trip because there hasn't been any discussion up until now. She asks him why he has broached this topic, but already suspects that it relates to money concerns. Sure enough, she's right, and she reacts to Ken's comments with anger.

Both Kim and Ken are only focused upon their own issues and emotions. Ken is worried about finances, and instead of telling Kim about this concern, he suggests that she cancel her trip. When she takes this badly, he doesn't acknowledge her surprise or upset. He senses Kim's annoyed, but doesn't tune into her feeling, as he's determined to push ahead with his serious agenda.

Kim is surprised, but doesn't give any thought as to why Ken is telling her to skip her trip. Her own annoyance takes centre stage, and she expresses her anger. Ken's worry isn't acknowledged because Kim is too busy being angry. This isn't a new issue; it has come up many times before in relation to different matters.

TEAM TOOLS

Ken's and Kim's own feelings have caused them to react to each other and stifle further discussion.

Bringing up an issue before it creates a lot of worry can be more productive than avoiding the issue and having it surface later in an inflammatory fashion. It can be very difficult to listen when one is full of one's own feelings about an issue.

Ken can bring up his worry before it becomes too overwhelming. In this way, it will be easier for him to speak in a non-confrontational fashion; at the same time, it will be easier for Kim to hear him without her feelings taking over. This can be tough to do when the topic is a sensitive one, but the likelihood of good collaboration is enhanced.

Learning to listen:

Ken: *"I'm really worried about our finances right now."*
Kim: *"This isn't a new concern for you."*
Ken: *"I know, but some extra bills have come up that have broken the bank, so to speak."*
Kim: *"Are you saying you don't want me to go to the Island?"*
Ken: *"I know you really want to go, so maybe you and I could find ways*

to pinch pennies in other areas."

Kim: *"You have been looking preoccupied lately. Let's sit in the kitchen and I'll put the tea on."*

TIP: Holding on to issues can create a "build'n'blow" situation.

Little Boy Listening

Ken is trying to be more positive about finances.

Ken: *"I think we can take some savings and purchase the RV we've been talking about. It would allow us to get out on the road and see some of this country of ours."*
Kim: *"It would be exciting to head up north."*
Ken: *"It sure would. We could even take out some cash for some motor-bikes that we could carry on the back of the unit."*
Kim: *(Sits quietly and seems tense)*
Ken: *"You can get these smaller units that would be great for zipping around after we set up camp."*
Kim: *(Appears more tense and says nothing)*
Ken: *"I even thought about getting a little trailer to tow the bikes."*

WHAT is happening here?

Ken is doing something he finds hard to do. He's thinking out loud with Kim, and after some initial awkwardness, is getting right into it. He notices that Kim seems tense, but he keeps on going with his train of thought.

Opening up is a big step for Ken, as he doesn't often speak much out of fear of upsetting Kim. His "little boy thought" about tension is that it must be avoided. He thinks that if he ignores the tension, it will go away.

TEAM TOOLS

Most spouses are very good at picking up on each other's feelings. However, these feelings may be intimidating for one or both of them.

Ken can continue to express his ideas to Kim. However, he can also practise listening while he's speaking. When a feeling arises in a discussion, it needs to take centre stage. Good perception can lead to acknowledging and accepting the feelings of the other person.

Here's another way the above conversation could have unfolded:

Ken: *"I think we can take some savings and purchase the RV we've been talking about. It would allow us to get out on the road and see some of this country of ours."*
Kim: *"It would be exciting to head up north."*
Ken: *"It sure would. We could even take out some cash for some motorbikes that we could carry on the back of the unit."*
Kim: *(Sits quietly and seems tense)*
Ken: *"You don't seem very enthused with this plan."*
Kim: *"Well, you know me. I don't feel that comfortable with motorbikes."*
Ken: *"The bikes might be pushing it a bit?"*
Kim: *"I think so."*
Ken: *"You're probably right. Maybe we can work out some other arrangements."*

TIP: When a feeling shows up in a conversation, it should become the focus.

She's Not Listening to Me

Ken is venting to Kim about his frustration with some work issues.

Ken: *"The overtime at work is really starting to wear me down."*
Kim: *"Have you thought of talking to your boss?"*
Ken: *"That won't help. He's never around anyway. He doesn't care. The other thing that annoys me a lot is that the sales reps are always going off for meetings!"*
Kim: *(Says nothing and looks distracted)*
Ken: *"You never listen to me when I talk about my day!"* *(Withdraws)*

WHAT is *happening here*?

Ken is concentrating on sharing his concerns with his wife. He has no sense of the impact upon her. Kim isn't listening to him the way he wants her to, and this offends him. It doesn't occur to him that she also has feelings, and that it might be wise to pause and ask her how she is.

TEAM TOOLS

Sometimes a listener will offer advice right away if she's feeling uncomfortable with what she's hearing. It is an attempt to fix the problem and make it go away.

When talking with another person, keep in mind that their feelings and thoughts are equally important. There's a good chance your words may be having an impact on the listener.

Ken can share his day and monitor the impact upon Kim. If she's not tuning in the way he wants, or seems distracted, it may be because she's upset by what Ken is sharing.

Your Turn...

(Cover the section below and write on a note pad how you might resolve this issue.)

Ken: *"The overtime at work is really starting to wear me down."*
Kim: *"Have you thought of talking to your boss?"*
Ken: *"That won't help. Do you find it hard to hear me go on and on about work?"*

Kim: *"It frustrates me the way they treat you. I'd like to go down there and tell a few people what I think!"*

Ken: *"It frustrates me too. Would you rather I didn't tell you so much?"*

Kim: *"No, I'm fine. I'll try to just listen to your concerns without getting so worked up."*

TIP: **Listen always, even when talking.**

Judge Not

Ken is sharing with Kim once again, and notices that she's responding by giving him some suggestions. She knows how to listen with empathy and without giving advice, but she's telling him her ideas. He pauses and asks her if what he's saying bothers her. She says "No," but that she thinks his concern is "ridiculous" because the issue is so trivial.

WHAT is happening here?

Kim is evaluating the issue that is upsetting Ken. By doing this, she offends him.

> **TEAM TOOLS**
>
> Kim judges Ken's frustrations as relatively insignificant. Nevertheless, she can decide to be patient and understanding as she listens attentively and reflects on how frustrated he must feel.
>
> By using this approach, Ken will feel understood and supported, and much less likely to be frustrated by similar events in the future.
>
> When listening to another person about a heated topic, it doesn't matter whether the listener agrees with the significance of the issue discussed. The focus needs to be on the feelings of the speaker, regardless of what the issue is.

Learning to listen:

Ken: *"The interruptions at the office make it hard for me to concentrate."*

Kim: *"Does that frustrate you?"*

Ken: *"Yes it does, and it worries me as well because I am behind in my writing."*

Kim: *(thinks to herself that she would push ahead despite interruptions, but sets this thought aside to listen to Ken)* *"It sounds like you're feeling a lot of pressure."*

TIP: Judging can get in the way of good listening.

OSSIE AND OLIVIA

Independent though they are, Ossie and Olivia have opened up more to each other's interests. They also have different parenting styles, and can sometimes power struggle around their differences and the feelings that go with them.

Who's Defensive?

Ossie is telling Olivia about an incident with their daughter and he notices that Olivia is upset. He asks her what's wrong and she says that she thinks he may have been too hard on their daughter. Ossie then repeats what he was saying in an attempt to explain himself. Olivia tells him that he doesn't need to be defensive.

WHAT is happening here?

Ossie notices that Olivia is unhappy with what he's saying, and rather than simply asking her if she's upset, he asks her what's wrong.

Olivia hears his story, but is caught up in her own feelings. She completely misses Ossie's concerns about the incident with their daughter. When he repeats himself, she accuses him of being defensive, which he then denies.

TEAM TOOLS

When Ossie senses that Olivia is upset, instead of attempting to clarify what was intended, he can acknowledge and accept Olivia's feelings. Olivia can do the same for him. In this way, there will be a productive sharing of ideas.

It is always important to acknowledge the feelings generated by a discussion of family-related issues. This makes it easier to focus on the various issues at hand. All the while, it's crucial to keep checking on other feelings that may arise during such a discussion.

In the following conversation, Olivia manages to not be overwhelmed by her own upset, and tunes into Ossie. In so doing, she's surprised with what he has to say. Ossie is also able to show his own feelings.

Learning to listen:

As Ossie tells Olivia about an another incident with their daughter, Olivia starts to feel upset, but manages to ask Ossie if he's feeling bothered by what happened with their teen. Olivia has learned that if she's feeling agitated about an incident or an account of that incident, there's a good chance that Ossie also feels bothered by it. She also knows that Ossie has been frustrated with their daughter lately. Ossie confirms that he is, and that he feels helpless as well. Ossie and Olivia now discuss possible future interventions.

TIP: *Acknowledge feelings frequently.*

RON AND ROSA

Ron and Rosa are considering marriage and are dealing with unresolved family issues. They are learning how to heal old wounds and to listen to each other more effectively. These attempts extend to their interactions with their respective families.

She Loves Her More

Ron and his mother are discussing his sister's alcohol addiction.

Ron: *"I'm really angry with Colleen. She's been behaving really poorly and it's not fair to Colin and the kids"*
Mom: *"You don't know the whole story. She does some things right."*
Ron: *"There you go, taking her side again."*
Mom: *"I'm not taking her side. I know she has problems."*
Ron: *"You always defend her!"*

WHAT is happening here?

Ron is angry with his mother for defending his sister. However, he's not aware of how his mother is feeling while listening to his complaints. It sounds like his mother is defending Colleen, but Ron doesn't look deeper. His mother reacts to Ron's words by feeling guilty, and he reacts to her words by feeling offended. No one is listening.

TEAM TOOLS

Rather than reacting, Ron and his mother can listen to and address the feelings behind each other's words. In this way, the conversation can reach a deeper level. They both may discover that there are numerous emotions "lurking in the weeds."

Learning to listen:

Ron: *"Does it bother you when I talk about Colleen?"*
Mom: *"Well, I feel guilty when I hear you talk like that. I think it's my fault she's turned out the way she has."*
Ron: *"I don't want you to feel guilty, and I don't think it's your fault."*
Mom: *"You seem really angry with her."*
Ron: *"Well, I am angry, but I'm mostly worried. Maybe even scared for her."*
Mom: *"I'm scared for her as well."*

TIP: *Personal feelings can take over and get in the way of hearing the other person.*

I Heard You the First Time

Ron is talking about his day and he mentions that some issues at work bother him. He gives some examples to Rosa, who listens quietly. Rosa seems intent on listening to Ron and understanding his issues, but she is, by nature, on the quiet side.

Ron finishes his story, pauses, and then launches into it again. He goes through the entire story and when he's done, he pauses briefly, and begins it for the third time. Half way through the third telling, Ron notices that Rosa is looking away and appears to be distracted. He feels hurt and angry, and breaks off with a comment about her not being interested in his story.

WHAT *is happening here?*

Rosa is listening to Ron, and hears his frustration. She nods once or twice, but doesn't give him feedback. She doesn't ask him if he's frustrated or annoyed with his workmates; she just continues to listen quietly.

Ron appreciates the nods from Rosa, but because he doesn't hear anything from her, he assumes that she hasn't heard him, which makes him feel the need to tell the story again. Note that he does not ask her what she thinks or if she has heard him. After the second telling, he assumes the same thing and launches into his story yet again.

Rosa is becoming frustrated, as she heard and understood the first time, and she begins to tune out. Ron picks up on the "tuning out" and accuses Rosa of disinterest. In this situation, no feedback leads to repetitive sharing and frustration all around!

TEAM TOOLS

Silently picking up on the mood and ideas of a speaker but not saying anything doesn't help that person feel heard or understood. (As mentioned above with Gord and Gina, there can be exceptions to this rule).

Rosa can learn that not only does she have to listen, she has to prove it from time to time by giving Ron feedback. If she asks him whether he's feeling a certain way, he won't need to repeat himself, and will move on to other topics more quickly. Even if the feedback isn't accurate in terms of the exact feeling, Ron can clarify what the actual feeling is, and then move on.

Learning to listen:

Ron: *"That new rule at work about not talking on the phone between ten and noon isn't working. Several people are ignoring the rule and the supervisor isn't saying anything!"*
Rosa: *"Does it frustrate you when the supervisor ignores the situation?"*
Ron: *"Yes, it sure does. Actually, the rule itself is sort of useless, if you ask me."*
Rosa: *"Maybe the supervisor feels the same way."*
Ron: *"Then he shouldn't have made up the rule in the first place."*
Rosa: *"I can see how that would be annoying."*
Ron: *"Oh well. It's ultimately his problem, I guess. How are you doing?"*

TIP: Feedback helps a speaker feel heard.

SUSAN AND STAN

Susan used to readily express her anger and has now swung to the other extreme. She can still become upset, but is very cautious about speaking her mind. After a time apart from Susan, Stan realized he wanted to save their marriage, but didn't want to return to his old reserved role.

From Anger to Fear to Acceptance

It is morning and everyone is getting ready for work or school. Susan and

Stan's son, Billy, is taking his time and ignoring his father's requests to move quickly. Stan becomes impatient and starts to yell at his son. Susan sees this interaction while she is helping their daughter get her school books together.

WHAT is happening here?

In the past, Susan would have challenged Stan and expressed annoyance with his attitude towards Billy. But now she decides not to say anything because she fears upsetting him. Susan has gone from being angry with Stan's moods to being fearful and reticent.

Susan is afraid that if she speaks up, Stan may reconsider returning to the marriage. She knows that the old "blast him" approach doesn't work, and now she's fearful of making any comment.

TEAM TOOLS

Fear can get in the way of open communication and teamwork. When a certain approach or pattern of communication doesn't work, it's easy to swing to the opposite extreme.

Susan can work up the nerve to be more open with Stan when he appears to be angry or upset. She can give a clear message about her feelings, which affirms Stan's at the same time. Susan can also wait until later to ask Stan if he was annoyed with Billy, and then offer her advice at that time.

Learning to listen:

Stan: *"Hurry up, Billy. Let's get going!"*
Billy: *(Ignores his father)*
Stan: *(loudly)* *"I told you to get MOVING!"*
Susan: *"Billy, it's frustrating for me and your Dad when you drag your feet."*
Billy: *"Okay, okay."*

TIP: Listening takes courage

Tone Sensitive

Stan and Susan are driving into the city for a night at the opera. Susan is talking about a call from Stan's mother and she sounds edgy. Stan is annoyed, and he tells her not to use that tone with him. Susan denies that she's using any tone, and becomes annoyed herself. Stan is irritated that Susan is ignoring his concern and also denying how she sounds (which is so obvious to him!)

WHAT *is happening here?*

Stan is very sensitive to Susan using "tones" with him, as this seems to him like a "put-down." He used to keep his upset feelings to himself, but since his separation, he's more open with his concerns. It even occurs to him that Susan is intentionally trying to irritate him. Susan, as it happens, isn't intent on annoying Stan. She is simply upset with her own day and is trying to share it.

TEAM TOOLS

Reactionary listening occurs when the listener is caught up in his or her own feelings about what is being heard.

Stan can sense that Susan is upset, stop the conversation, and tentatively acknowledge the upset by guessing what she may be feeling. He can, for example, ask her if she was bothered by the call. When a feeling is acknowledged and accepted, it can open up discussion, which leads to further insights.

Learning to listen:

Stan asks Susan if the call bothered her, and she says that it did. She goes on to mention some topics that came up, and Stan asks her if she's angry with his mother. Susan says that she's not so much angry as frustrated, and perhaps a little worried about Stan's mother developing dementia. Stan asks Susan to tell him more, and after sharing her feelings, Susan feels heard and respected.

TIP: *Reactionary listening often begets reactionary listening.*

TOM AND TINA

Tom and Tina both continue to work full time while raising three children. They have little energy for time alone together, but have been trying to make this a priority. Their personality differences create some tension from time to time.

She's On Her Own

Tom and Tina are having a talk about parenting and the exchange of ideas has been productive. However, they come to an issue about which they disagree, and Tom speaks his mind forcefully. There is an interruption as the children appear on the scene with some questions. After the kids have left, Tom notices that Tina is quiet. He leaves her be.

WHAT *is happening here?*

Frustration with Tina's communication style leads to a missed opportunity for Tom to reach out to her. A productive conversation is stalled because one of the participants has become tense and quiet. Tom, in this case, has no trouble perceiving his wife's feelings, but rather than checking them out, he withdraws from the discussion.

TEAM TOOLS

It can be easy to leave all the responsibility for sharing feelings with the other person. It is acceptable for Tom to expect Tina to speak up if she has something to say. However, he could help her out by asking her how she's doing. Tina's fear of an argument causes her to hold back.

Tom's perception of Tina's feelings is accurate. He can not only ask Tina about her mood, but can also accept what he hears, and invite her to participate in a constructive discussion.

Your Turn...

(Cover the section below and write on a note pad how you might resolve this issue.)

Later on in the evening Tom notices that Tina is still quiet. He asks if she's upset about something he said earlier. She says that she's worried about one of his strategies, as she thinks it might be too tough on the kids. Tom is surprised, but is open to hearing Tina's alternative idea and the conversation continues with both spouses feeling less tense.

TIP: **Help your spouse to communicate by listening well.**

Non-Verbal Shot

Tom and Tina are talking about their son, Timmy.

Tom: *"You are too lenient with Timmy!"*
Tina: *(Makes a face and rolls her eyes)*
Tom: *"There you go, giving me attitude again."*
Tina: *"What are you talking about?"*

WHAT is happening here?

Tom and Tina have talked about this issue before. They differ in their parenting styles, and at times, are critical of one another. Tom is making an accusation instead of raising the topic in a more neutral fashion, such as: "Can we talk about Timmy?" Tom is very observant and notices Tina's facial expression right away. However, instead of asking her if she's upset, he assumes the worst and attacks.

TEAM TOOLS

Tina may not even realize that she has made a face. However, she's aware that this topic is a sensitive one for Tom. His accusing attitude tips her off that he's upset about something.

Tina can ask Tom if he's annoyed instead of making a "here we go again" face. Empathic listening can open up a discussion instead of starting a fight. Tina, in the following discussion, listens well by not allowing her husband's accusation to set her off. She can sense that he's upset, and asks him for clarification; then she's able to respond in a way that clears up the concern.

Here is another way the above story could have unfolded:

Tom: *"You are too lenient with Timmy!"*

Tina: *"Have I done something that bothers you?"*

Tom: *"Yes. I thought we made a deal with him that there'll be no TV until his homework is done."*

Tina: *"We did make that deal, but I gave him a break tonight as he had a big test today, and he wants to take the night off."*

Tom: *"That seems fair, I guess."*

TIP: Listen with empathy.

Another Non-Verbal Shot

Tom: *"Timmy isn't doing his homework again. I think we're going to have to sit him down and have a chat."*

Tina: *"I thought he was doing better with school."*

Tom: *"That was last term. Lately, he's been on the Internet all the time, and nothing is getting done. He's really starting to annoy me with his attitude!"*

Tina: *(Smiles)*

Tom: *"What's so funny? I hate it when you make fun of me!"*

Tina: *"I'm not making fun of you."*

Tom: *(angrily) "Don't give me that. I can see the smirk on your face!"*

WHAT is happening here?

Tina is surprised that Tom is upset, as she thought things were better between them. Tom goes on to clarify his concern and his feelings rise, with annoyance surfacing first.

Tina doesn't like conflict. She smiles when she gets nervous. Tom interprets the smile as a smirk, and assumes that he's being put down in some way. It doesn't occur to him to ask Tina if she is indeed amused. He assumes she's mocking him, and he attacks.

Tina is feeling tense and isn't aware that she smiles when she's anxious. She can see that Tom has misinterpreted her expression, as she wasn't trying to mock him. Rather than ask Tom if he's upset, she tries to defend herself without mentioning that she's tense about his being annoyed with their son. Tina is protective of Timmy because she thinks Tom is too hard on him.

TEAM TOOLS

Assumptions happen all the time and may get us into trouble if they are not checked out. Tom knows that parenting is a sensitive topic for him and his wife. Tina is easy-going and finds it hard to play the "bad cop" role. Tom recalls other times when she had been nervous and smiled in response. He is frustrated in this situation, and finds it hard to listen.

They can both learn to respond differently to each other. For example, Tina can allow her husband his upset, and Tom can enquire about her smile, as he suspects she may be uncomfortable with his anger.

Here is another way the above story could have unfolded:

Tina: *"I thought Timmy was doing better with school."*
Tom: *"That was last term. Lately, he's been on the Internet all the time and nothing is getting done. He's really starting to annoy me with his attitude!"*
Tina: *"I know his Internet habits bother you."*
Tom: *"I just worry that his grades won't be good enough for college."*

Or

Tina: *(Smiles)*
Tom: *"Does my anger with Timmy bother you?"*
Tina: *"Well, I don't like to see you upset. I know he's been pushing the limits a bit of late, but I think he's still getting a lot done during his spare blocks at school."*

Tom: *"I hope he is. Will you ask him about it? I don't want him to think I'm a nag about school."*

TIP: Unchecked assumptions lead to misunderstandings.

He's So Defensive

Tom and Tina are driving to a weekend getaway. In general, Tina has been opening up more with Tom and telling him what bothers her. She notices after a short time that he seems agitated and defensive. She finds this frustrating, and stops talking to him about her concerns. They sit together in silence for the rest of the drive.

WHAT *is happening here?*

It is good that Tina is trying to be more open with Tom, as she's been hesitant to do this in the past. She raises a couple of concerns, but unfortunately, doesn't first ask him about his day or his current mood.

Rather than accept her concerns, Tom withdraws, feeling attacked. Not feeling understood, Tina shuts down. Neither acknowledges the other's feeling.

> **TEAM TOOLS**
>
> When talking with Tom, it's important for Tina to monitor his reaction and to ask about his feelings. Often, feelings may present themselves in a disconcerting way (e.g. defensiveness). For his part, Tom has the challenge of not getting caught up in his own feelings about what Tina has said. He can ask Tina if she's concerned or annoyed.

Your Turn...

(Cover the section below and write on a note pad how you might resolve this issue.)

Tom and Tina are driving to a weekend getaway. In general, Tina has been opening up more with Tom. She begins their conversation by asking how he is. He seems tired to her, and she asks him if this is the case. It turns out that he is, but he's excited to be having a weekend away without the kids.

He asks her if she's fine, and she says she's a little frustrated with the job list from the last week. Tom acknowledges her annoyance and says that he'll get back on task early in the week. Tina says she hopes she's not bothering him by bringing up her concerns.

TIP: Feelings are hiding behind defensiveness.

"Let's review the Tips..."

• Accept the feelings of another person.

• Acceptance leads to greater openness.

• Checking out feelings first makes for better listening.

• Listening but not commenting is appropriate at times.

• Hear the feelings behind the words.

• Changing the subject may indicate underlying discomfort.

• Listen first, clarify second and then listen some more.

• Checking out a tone of voice is better than reacting to it.

• Good listening leads to good listening.

• Holding on to issues can create a build'n'blow situation.

• When a feeling shows up in a conversation, it should become the focus.

• Listen always, even when talking.

• Judging can get in the way of good listening.

• Acknowledge feelings frequently.

• Personal feelings can take over and get in the way of hearing the other person.

• Feedback helps a speaker feel heard.

• Listening takes courage.

- Reactionary listening often begets reactionary listening.
- Help your spouse to communicate by listening well.
- Listen with empathy.
- Unchecked assumptions lead to misunderstandings.
- Feelings are hiding behind defensiveness.

CHAPTER SEVEN

Consultation & Collaboration

Consultation and collaboration comprise the business portion of the T-Time (Daily Talk-Time). It is a time to discuss issues of mutual concern and offer personal perspectives.

Individuals are attracted to each other for a variety of reasons. During a courtship, each person attempts to appear similar to the other, even emphasizing all the interests each has "in common." Differences are often downplayed, ignored, or expected to change after marriage. Other times, they are admired. It may happen that after marriage, a couple will discover that two very unique persons are now married to each other, and that conflicts are not readily resolved.

One spouse may be a "saver" and the other a "spender"; one a strict parent and the other more easy going; one emotional, the other rational. The list goes on. Before a marriage, the contrasting traits may be admired. A spender may have respected the saver's ability to manage money, but now that the marriage has begun, there is a change in perspective. If the couple don't collaborate (and this often results from weak or non-existent daily talks or T-Times), then the previously admired qualities are now resented. The "saver" may now appear to be stingy in the eyes of the other partner.

If a couple enter a discussion aware that the final solution will be collaboration, there's a more relaxed atmosphere. There's less of a tendency to compete or argue about differences (power struggles where both spouses lose). Often, the "give and take" can lead to a decision or plan that is superior to what either individual would have come up with alone.

Also, each partner learns from the other. A strict parent will move towards a more relaxed approach through the collaboration, and the easygoing parent will become firmer through working as a team.

Collaboration is not simply "caving in" to the other's ideas so as to avoid disputes. Each spouse must listen to the other's feelings and ideas as a first step in creating a genuine collaboration.

Unless married couples are prepared to seek a good consensus through consultation, serious disagreements could result. If a marriage is to be great or to avoid "singing the blues", the participants must place a high value on joint decision-making.

At times, staunch individualists decry such thinking. A marriage, however, is a union of two "selves" and for it to survive and thrive, neither person can be superior. To put it another way, marriage is an opportunity to become more selfless and caring. A major cause of divorce is too much self-centeredness.

As children, we are dependent, and as adults, we grow into greater independence. But sometimes, adult independence is valued to the point where partners resist developing a healthy sense of interdependence.

Some people fear the loss of their individuality within marriage. The paradox, however, is fascinating. Each individual will gain a renewed sense of self-worth when they consult, collaborate, and make their relationship the priority.

It may be that everyone has the same potential ability to be open or closed, neat or sloppy and so on. When a couple meet, they assess each other, and if one is outgoing, perhaps the other pulls back and becomes more quiet on occasion, or vice versa. Perhaps differences in behaviour are simply adjustments each person makes in a subconscious attempt to balance out the other.

Couples who realize that the strengths of each partner are potential resources rather than annoyances will feel more comfortable consulting and collaborating. Everyone has psychological blind spots and frequently each spouse can see where the other is blind. Consultation can open up broader perspectives and the resulting collaboration will be a more informed and thoughtful solution to a challenge.

BOB AND BETH

This couple are improving with their communication as they adjust to their new life as a married couple. Bob is the more open of the two, but he can be selective about what he shares with Beth.

Dinner Party Surprise

Bob and Beth are attending a dinner party with good friends and the conversation has moved to work issues. Bob tells their hosts about some changes at work and it is a shock for Beth. She hasn't heard this information before, even though Bob has known about it for some time. She's hurt that he hasn't told her about these changes before bringing them up at the dinner party.

WHAT *is happening here?*

Bob and Beth are busy with their jobs and other commitments, and there isn't always time to chat. When they do make the time, they don't go into much detail about their work. Bob tries to leave his work at work.

TEAM TOOLS

Regular consultation helps couples keep up-to-date with each other's lives. Regular T-Times involve talking about each other's day to some degree. The focus isn't on what's done during a day at work so much as what the work day did to the person. Such conversation will lead to each spouse sharing information with the other before sharing it with family and friends. There will be no more dinner party surprises!

Learning to consult:

On their way to a sporting event with friends, Bob tells them about the illness of one of his colleagues. Beth has heard this information before, as she and Bob had discussed it during a recent T-Time. She is able to share her thoughts and reactions when asked by their friends.

TIP: Share information with your spouse before sharing it with friends.

Saturday Morning Battles

Bob and Beth are spending their Saturday morning hanging out together and running errands. Bob makes a list of his errands and projects, and after their breakfast, they head off, with Beth driving.

On this particular day, Beth decides she wants to drop by a music store to pick up a gift for her sister. Bob is annoyed because the music store isn't on his list and there are other places to visit. Beth doesn't have a list. She has a few plans in her mind, and one of them is to get a CD for her sister. She's irritated with Bob for making a fuss about her stopping. Bob is annoyed that his list is being ignored.

WHAT is happening here?

This couple are attempting to spend some time together, and in many ways it works well for them. They run into trouble, however, because although they are traveling together, they have separate agendas for the morning. It's only a matter of time before the two plans clash.

TEAM TOOLS

It's great that this couple want to share their Saturday mornings. If there are two opinions about how to spend time together, it's helpful to create a third, collaborative option.

Learning to collaborate:

The next Saturday, Bob makes a list of his errands and projects and Beth does the same. She usually doesn't make lists, but has agreed to do so. After their meal they compare lists, create a joint one, map the route, and then head off.

There are no hassles when they run their errands because they are working from a collaborative list and both sets of expectations are being met. Because the morning goes so well, there is no tension if one or the other wants to make an impromptu change in "their plan."

TIP: Move from my way to our way.

HARVEY AND HANNA

Harvey is overcoming his shyness and discomfort with opening up. He has swung to the other extreme by speaking his mind more openly, and in the process, forgets from time to time that collaboration is their goal.

Differences Are Fine

Harvey and Hanna are talking about their summer holiday. Harvey wants to plan a route that will involve covering a lot of distance in a short period of time. His plan is an ambitious attempt to see a large section of the province.

Hanna finds it stressful to be travelling so much on a holiday. She wants to go to a lake, rent a cabin, and stay put for two weeks. Harvey tells Hanna that her plan is boring. Hanna tells Harvey his plan is exhausting to think about, let alone actually do.

WHAT is happening here?

This couple is trying to plan their holiday and some typically opposing points of view are expressed. Both spouses have reasons why they don't like the other person's plan, and the discussion is about to become an argument.

TEAM TOOLS

Differences in personality and ideas are normal and even valuable. The value comes from each person having access to a fuller perspective through the eyes of the other.

The danger is that spouses can forget about trying to collaborate, and instead, become entrenched in a power struggle. This may happen because they forget that they don't have to stretch all the way over to the other person's perspective; they only need to meet in the middle. However, there may be times when stretching over is fine, especially when one idea has merit.

This couple have come to appreciate their differences. They used to be concerned about them and even argue in an attempt to make the other agree. They aren't concerned any longer, and can even joke about how predictably predictable they can be with each other.

In this case, two itineraries are on the table. They have a starting point. Neither Harvey nor Hanna is locked into having their way, as they understand that some sort of joint plan is in order.

They may joke around a little with a mock debate about how great each individual perspective is. Then they can move on to a joint plan for their summer trip. The collaborative process enriches the relationship.

Learning to collaborate:

Hanna and Harvey decide on a plan whereby they tour for a week and see an area of the province they haven't seen before. Then they will stay at a cabin on a favourite lake and take it easy for their second week of holidays.

TIP: *Collaborate to enrich your marriage.*

KEN AND KIM

Ken has been more open and assertive with Kim, and has learned to listen more effectively as well. Kim is also improving in her listening and not reacting to Ken's improved openness.

Birthday Party

Ken and Kim are celebrating their daughter's seventh birthday by throwing a party for her and her friends. Kim is organizing the girls, and Ken is trying to be helpful. He senses that Kim may be getting a little tired. The girls are finishing their lunch, and the cake hasn't yet been presented.

Ken announces to the girls that it would be good to take a break and go out to the yard for a few games. Kim interrupts Ken's announcement and tells them to stay put. Ken is embarrassed and withdraws.

WHAT is happening here?

Ken is trying to be more supportive of Kim, and for this reason, has stuck around to help out at the party. Kim appreciates his efforts and things proceed nicely. Ken notices that Kim is getting a little worn down, and he may be right. But instead of asking her how she's doing, he makes an assumption and acts on it.

TEAM TOOLS

It is important to consult about an idea. Helping is great, but doing it in a way that strengthens the marriage is also very important. Ken had good intentions, but is now hurt at having his efforts rejected. If he had taken Kim aside and consulted with her, the outcome may have been different.

Your Turn...

(Cover the section below and write on a note pad how you might resolve this issue.)

Ken takes Kim aside and asks her if she's getting tired. She says she is, but that she's fine. He suggests that the kids head outside to play for a while to give her a break. She says she would prefer they stay a little longer and eat their cake, as it will be too hard to get them back to the table once they begin to play. Ken and Kim return to the kitchen, and after everyone sings Happy Birthday and shares the cake, Ken invites the children out to the yard for some games.

TIP: *Consultation leads to joint plans.*

Ouch, but Thanks

Ken still finds it hard at times to open up with Kim. He isn't that articulate and dislikes conflict. Over time, Ken has learned that his health and marriage suffer when he and Kim don't talk enough. Kim is also aware of this problem, and occasionally pressures Ken to open up more.

Ken decides that he's going to tell Kim some things he dislikes about the way she manages their home and finances. When he does, she gets upset. Ken becomes uncomfortable and is tempted to shut down and keep his ideas to himself.

WHAT is happening here?

This couple are improving their marriage through greater openness and better listening. Ken is braver in his talking than he has ever been in the past. Previously, there had been times when Kim sensed that something was wrong, but Ken didn't say anything.

Ken is finding it easier to open up, as Kim is listening more effectively. In this instance, she's upset by what she hears, and lets Ken know she is annoyed.

TEAM TOOLS

Opening up dialogue between spouses can be valuable, even if it's hard to hear at times. The reserved spouse has to work on opening up, and the more talkative one needs to focus on listening instead of jumping in with a response.

At the same time, the reserved spouse has to work on his listening so that he can monitor his spouse's reactions to what he says and allow for her feelings.

Because he's now opening up, there's the risk that Ken will ignore the impact upon his wife. He can speak his mind but listen as well. In the past, he was very tuned in to Kim's feelings. He

▌has now been concentrating on opening up more, but he can also monitor the impact upon Kim as he does so.

Your Turn...

(Cover the section below and write on a note pad how you might resolve this issue.)

Ken tells Kim some things he dislikes about the way she manages their home and finances and she gets upset, but she realizes how hard it is for Ken to speak his mind. It's good that he's being more open, as this allows her imagination to take a break. When he didn't open up in the past, she spent a lot of time trying to figure out his feelings.

Ken notices Kim's unhappiness with his feedback and this makes him uncomfortable. But instead of shutting down or blindly pushing ahead, this time he checks out her feelings. She tells him that she's upset, but is glad that he's sharing his concerns with her.

TIP: Watch for the impact of your words on the other person.

OSSIE AND OLIVIA

This couple continues to struggle with parenting issues.

Collaboration Doesn't Mean Appeasement or Caving In

Ossie and Olivia are talking about their daughter, Sandy's, curfew. Ossie is adamant that she be home by ten o'clock, which Olivia thinks is too early. She says that she prefers a later time. Ossie repeats his opinion with some irritation. Olivia is a little tired and is worried about a hassle, so she goes along with him.

A few days later, Sandy is an hour later than Ossie thinks she should be. Sandy is surprised when her dad gets upset. Before going out, she had spoken with her mother and Olivia hadn't mentioned the earlier time. Ossie is upset with Olivia for not supporting him with what he thought they had agreed was a new curfew.

WHAT *is happening here?*

Ossie and Olivia get full marks for trying to work out a joint plan. Olivia decides to agree with Ossie even though she would prefer a different curfew time. Later, because she isn't invested in the joint decision, Olivia forgets the new time when she's talking with her daughter. Ossie is annoyed because he believes that Olivia isn't following through on what "they" decided.

TEAM TOOLS

Olivia appeased Ossie rather than working out a good collaboration with him. For his part, Ossie didn't double-check with Olivia to see if she really was comfortable with the new arrangement.

Some spouses appear to agree to something but are only trying to avoid an argument. It's important to be open to each other's ideas and opinions.

The story continues:

Later in the week, Ossie and Sandy are again talking about curfews, and Sandy becomes frustrated and upset. She asks her mother for help, and Olivia tells her to listen to her father. Olivia feels guilty for siding with Ossie as she doesn't agree with the rule.

WHAT *is happening here?*

To avoid another hassle, Olivia decides to cave in. Because of her fear, she sticks to this plan in spite of her own guilt and belief that Ossie is too strict.

TEAM TOOLS

Olivia's approach isn't fair to her daughter, and Sandy may lose respect for her mother because she hasn't stood up for what she believes in. When Ossie is away, she may allow Sandy to stay out, but will tell her not to tell her father. This would be a divisive and disrespectful thing to do.

When one parent gives in to the other because of fear of upset or conflict, the fairness of the parenting strategy is in jeopardy. When couples "work the middle," the result is often excellent psychology.

Learning to consult and collaborate:

Ossie and Olivia are talking about their daughter's curfew. Olivia is a little tired and is worried about a hassle, but asks Ossie if it bothers him that she disagrees with him. He says that he's frustrated because he thinks Sandy is too young to have a later time. He admits that he may be worrying too much.

Olivia says that she worries too, but that she thinks they need to be fair to Sandy, as most of her friends have a midnight curfew. They talk it over a little more and decide to agree on the later time on a trial basis only.

TIP: *Collaboration means to meet in the middle.*

STAN AND SUSAN

Stan and Susan continue to rebuild their intimacy after some rocky times. Stan is more open and Susan is less cautious. There is a healthier level of interaction between them, but tensions still arise from time to time.

The Listening Is Fine

Stan and Susan are talking about an upcoming renovation to their home. They are both excited about the project, and the current focus is the living room. Stan wants to add a sliding door and deck and he proposes this. Susan says that she thinks a deck would fit better off the family room. Stan becomes flustered with Susan, and accuses her of not listening to him.

WHAT *is happening here?*

Stan and Susan have a difference of opinion on the matter of a new deck. Stan becomes frustrated, as he thinks that Susan isn't listening to him. She is. She is just disagreeing with his idea, and gives her own opinion.

TEAM TOOLS

When a person doesn't seem to be listening, it may be that she is indeed listening but is disagreeing with the idea presented. The collaborative process can break down if both spouses get caught up in their perspective and don't listen to and accept each other's thoughts and feelings that accompany the topic.

Before there can be a collaborative decision, there needs to be a clear understanding of each person's starting position on an issue.

Learning to consult and collaborate:

Susan asks Stan if it frustrates him that she doesn't agree with his plan. He agrees that it does, but says he's mostly tired from a busy week. He suggests they take a break from their talk and go for a walk.

TIP: When your spouse seems not to be listening it may be that she is disagreeing.

TOM AND TINA

This couple have learned to make their marriage a priority, but they have busy lives. Parenting and work activities have taken over, and in spite of good intentions, Tom and Tina have drifted apart.

Are We Compatible?

Tom and Tina are going for marriage counselling as they are having some difficulties resolving contentious issues. Tom likes to talk about his day and Tina doesn't. Tom is big on saving money for the future, and Tina likes to live for today. This couple has three children and Tom is strict with them, whereas Tina is easygoing.

The counsellor tells this couple that they are too different and shouldn't be together. He says they aren't compatible because they are disagreeing in so many areas. Tom and Tina are shocked by the advice, and decide to seek another opinion.

WHAT is happening here?

Tom and Tina are a fairly typical couple. They are different in many ways and similar in a few. They have good balance. They are having trouble with each other not because of their differences (or similarities for that matter; i.e. strength of character), but because they still don't know how to work together or do business with each other.

TEAM TOOLS

Couples who do well in their marriages not only consult with each other, they also "work their differences." They do this by expressing their points of view and then moving to a collaborative position.

Counsellors and psychologists can be of immense help by showing a couple how to move beyond their differences to collaborative decision-making. Tom and Tina have enough sense to seek a second opinion.

Learning to consult and collaborate:

The new counsellor tells this couple that they are an excellent match and have great potential for good collaborative decision-making. He shows them how to do a T-Time so that they can ease their stress and build their unity as a couple. Upon this foundation, they will then learn to "do business" with each other.

TIP: Differences make for balance in a relationship.

VERONICA AND VINCE

This couple have recovered nicely from a short separation that gave Vince a huge wake-up call. Veronica is trying to be more assertive. Vince is making more time for his marriage and learning to listen as well.

Blind Spots and Bankruptcy

Vince and Veronica are feeling a lot of stress due to a business failure. Vince had gone into a new business with a fellow who turned out to be a crook. The partner left town with all the assets of the new company, and Vince and Veronica were forced into bankruptcy.

When Vince had been planning to go into business with this man he had taken him and his wife out to dinner with Veronica. Afterwards, Vince didn't ask Veronica what she thought of them. Veronica is a stay-at-home mom and perhaps because of this, he didn't see the value in checking out her impressions.

WHAT *is happening here?*

This couple is experiencing a lot of distress related to their lost business. Their retirement income had been invested in the venture, and they are losing their home. Veronica is angry with Vince even though she knows he's also upset.

TEAM TOOLS

There was no consultation between this couple because Vince assumed that Veronica wouldn't have something valuable to contribute. She isn't a business woman, but she does have good intuition and reads people very well. She is able to see where Vince is blind.

As mentioned previously everyone has psychological blind spots, things they can't see about themselves or others. Usually, each spouse is able to see where the other is blind. Vince was excited about having a new business partner, and dreamt of what the new company would look like. But he missed cues that might have tipped him off as to his new partner's reliability. Had the couple consulted about the new partner, Veronica's perspective would have saved the day.

Here is another way the above story could have unfolded:

Vince is planning to go into business with a new partner, and he takes Veronica out to dinner with this man and his wife. Following the dinner, he asks Veronica what she thought of them.

Veronica doesn't like the way the prospective partner treats his wife. Her intuition tells her that he's not trustworthy i.e. "He's not what he seems." Vince takes her opinion seriously, and makes the decision not to proceed with the partnership.

TIP: *Your spouse can see where you are blind.*

Looking for Love in All the Wrong Places

During a workshop for a large group of singles, participants were asked if they were looking for love. The general consensus was that they were.

They were asked to write a short list of the qualities they were looking for in a prospective spouse. They were then asked to write a short list of their own qualities. Finally, they were asked to read over the lists and compare them. The majority had written similar lists. They were looking for themselves!

TEAM TOOLS

Perhaps it's human nature to think that a suitable partner will be someone similar to oneself. Individuals who marry are similar in a few personality traits, such as strength of character (stubbornness), level of insecurity (woundedness, albeit shown in varying ways), and values. However, most spouses have different, and in many cases, opposite, personality characteristics or preferences. Such differences can make life more interesting and lead to mutual growth.

TIP: *Are you looking for yourself in a spouse?*

"Let's review the Tips..."

• Share information with your spouse before sharing it with friends.

• Move from my way to our way.

• Collaborate to enrich your marriage.

• Consultation leads to joint plans.

• Watch for the impact of your words on the other person.

• Collaboration means to meet in the middle.

• When your spouse seems not to be listening, it may be that she is disagreeing.

• Differences make for balance in a relationship.

• Your spouse can see where you are blind.

• Are you looking for yourself in a spouse?

CHAPTER EIGHT

Time-Out/Time-In

When it comes to anger, "getting out of hand" can take two paths. One is to blow up and rant and rave. The other is to shut down and withdraw. Both approaches are equally negative and ineffective ways of dealing with anger. Often a couple will display both approaches, depending on their different personalities.

The interesting thing is that when one partner blows up, it stresses out the other, less expressive person. When the quieter partner gets upset and withdraws, it upsets the more outgoing person. Each spouse is bothered by the anger style of the other.

Couples in great marriages know that anger can be dangerous. They also realize that when one spouse is becoming enraged at the other it means that neither one of them is listening effectively. Anticipating that such occasions may occur, some couples have a standing agreement to employ a "**Time-Out.**" Here are the rules:

> **Part One:** Either of you may call the Time-Out. Make sure that you have agreed beforehand that both of you will immediately stop talking about the sensitive topic when the Time-Out is called.

> **Part Two:** Cool down and give some thought as to what has happened. It is vital that each of you give some thought to **"what I could have done differently to prevent the destructive argument**." (Usually in this situation, each person thinks of a whole list of things the other person could have done differently! If the couple resumes their conversation with this attitude it will be like ringing a bell for "round two" of the original battle.)

> **Part Three:** Call a "**Time-In.**"(This is a very important part of the process.) One of you should only call a Time-In when you

know that your spouse is also ready. Often, one person is ready to talk sooner than the other. When you both agree to do the Time-In, each of you first shares some thoughts about what you could have done differently to help prevent the earlier skirmish. After this conversation you can then move on and discuss the original issues further.

KEN AND KIM

Both Ken and Kim have improved in their efforts to communicate more effectively, but there are times when old habits return. This can happen when one or both spouses are tired after a busy week.

"You Always Get Defensive!"

On this occasion, Ken and Kim are driving to a resort for a weekend away. The children are with relatives, and this is the first time in a long while that they have had a chance to escape on their own.

Ken: *(Driving quietly)*

Kim: *"I have a list of chores here I want to discuss with you."*

Ken: *(No comment, looks ahead, still concentrating on his driving.)*

Kim: *"These things never seem to get done."*

Ken: *(defensively)* *"I don't just sleep each weekend. I've been taking the kids to their sports."*

Kim: *"Yes you do, and you also watch your sports on the tube."*

Ken: *(slightly exasperated)* *"Don't I get to relax?"*

Kim: *(frustrated)* *"When do I get to relax? I never have time to watch my shows on TV!"*

Ken: *(Sits quietly)*

Kim: *(angrily)* *"Well you don't have to get defensive. You're always getting so defensive."*

Ken: *(No response)*

Kim: *(angrily)* *"Fine then! I don't care what you do!"*

Both ride on in a tense silence.

WHAT *is happening here?*

Ken is learning to open up more and often enjoys the T-Time with Kim. He finds it hard to stay with a discussion, however, if either of them becomes emotional. Ken, who considers himself a rational thinker, finds it hard to focus when Kim becomes upset or angry.

TEAM TOOLS

The Time-Out/Time-In strategy unfolds in seven steps:

Step One: Discuss the strategy in advance. Be sure to have a mutual agreement before using it.

Step Two: Create a code word. Feel free to use "Time-Out" or "T.O."

Step Three: Stop talking immediately about the sensitive topic when the Time-Out is called.

Step Four: Settle down and think about your personal role in the argument. Try not to focus on the faults of the other person.

Step Five: Call a Time-In. Only proceed if both spouses agree to do so.

Step Six: Start the discussion. Each person can focus on the role he or she played in the previous hassle.

Step Seven: Finish the original discussion.

Here is another way the above story could have unfolded using the Time-Out/Time-In strategy.

Ken: *(slightly exasperated)* *"Don't I get to relax?"*
Kim: *(frustrated)* *"When do I get to relax? I never have time to watch my shows on TV!"*

Ken: *"Time-Out."*

Later on in the drive, one or the other could offer to initiate a Time-In.

Ken called the Time-Out, but doesn't need to be the one to initiate the Time-In. In this case, he decides to be the initiator, and Kim is open to the invitation.

Ken: *"Would you like to try a Time-In?"*
Kim: *"Yes, I think so."*
Ken: *"Do you want to go first or should I?"*
Kim: *"I can start. The first thing that came to my mind about our conversation was my decision to start talking right away about business. I didn't ask you about your day or how you were. I sensed you were tired but didn't ask. I have to remember to check things out with you before getting down to business. The second thing I thought of was my reaction to what looked like your defensive behaviour. I think I got defensive right back, and then annoyed. I never paused to ask you if you were bothered with my bringing up my list. I think you probably were, and I must admit, my timing was off.*

Ken: *"Your raising the chore list right at the get-go took me by surprise. You must have been worried about it or you wouldn't have brought it up. I didn't ask you if you felt strongly about the chores. I was upset you chose that time to go into this business, and my annoyance sort of took over. I suppose I could have told you I was surprised and a bit annoyed with your timing. You're right about not checking in with each other. I was thinking about last week and didn't ask you how you were or if you were excited about getting away. The busyness of getting packed sort of threw me off, I guess. I'll get to the list when we get home and try to check one or two items off each weekend."*

Kim: *"I felt really uncomfortable after you called the Time-Out. It took me by surprise and then I realized I should have called it myself. Don't get me wrong about the chores thing. If some of them get done, I'd be happy. Maybe it would help if we set aside an hour or two on a Saturday and everyone did some chores at the same time.*

Ken: *"I like that idea. It would be good for the kids to learn to clean up more. Doing it at the same time will make it more enjoyable, if that's possible."*

TIP: Calling a Time-out prevents a power struggle.

MOLLY AND MARK

Mark is a strong money manager, whereas Molly is more easygoing. Mark doesn't like to argue, but he has been getting braver at bringing up his concerns. Molly doesn't mind a good debate, but she freezes up on the topic of money because she feels judged and criticized.

"You Drive Me Crazy!"

Mark: *"We need to discuss our budget. The credit card bill came in today, and as usual, we are way over!"*

Molly: *(sarcastically) "My day was fine thanks, how about yours?"*

Mark: *"This is important."*

Molly: *"I know it's important. But I haven't seen you all day and suddenly we're talking about your favourite topic: money!"*

Mark: *"You said you weren't going to use the credit card unless we discussed it first. What are these charges all about? This one at the hardware store, and this one at the restaurant?"*

Molly: *"I can't remember."*

Mark: *"Molly, you drive me crazy! I thought we had a deal."*

Molly: *"I don't want to talk about this right now. I've got other things on my mind."*

Mark: *"You never want to discuss anything. If you don't stop spending, we're going to go broke!"*

Molly: *"Mark, you always exaggerate so much. We're not going broke!"*

Mark: *(raised voice) "Here's another charge from the florist. When is this going to stop?"*

Molly: *(No response).*

Mark: *(raising his voice further)* *"Molly!"*

Molly: *(No response. Gets up from where she's sitting and leaves the room.)*

Mark: *(following Molly)* *"We're not finished here. You're avoiding my questions. Why not just answer me?"*

Molly: *(quietly)* *"We're finished."*

Using Time-Out/Time-In

Mark: *"We need to discuss our budget. The credit card bill came in today, and as usual, we're way over!"*

Molly: *(sarcastically)* *"My day was fine thanks, how about yours?"*

Mark: *"This is important."*

Molly: *"I know it's important. But I haven't seen you all day and suddenly we're talking about your favourite topic: money!"*

Mark: *"You said you weren't going to use the credit card unless we discussed it first. What are these charges all about? This one at the hardware store, and this one at the restaurant?"*

Molly: *"I can't remember. I just know they were both necessary."*

Mark: *"Molly, you drive me crazy. I thought we had a deal!"*

Molly: *"Time-Out."*

Both stop and the conversation ends. Mark leaves the room, and begins to do some work in his den. Molly decides to go for a walk.

Mark's thoughts:

"Why did she call a Time-Out? We were just getting started. She's using this Time-Out thing to avoid a sensitive topic. Alright, what's next here? Once a Time-Out is called, I'm supposed to think about where I blew it and talk about this with her. She's the spender; she's the one who blew it. Maybe I'd better calm down a little and think this through."

Ten minutes later, Mark refocuses on the discussion and thinks about what he could have done differently.

Molly's thoughts:

"He makes me so angry! All he ever thinks about is money. We didn't even hug and connect with one another when I came home. Right away, bang! We're into money talk. It hurts that he isn't more interested in my feelings. I'm too upset to think about the Time-In just now."

Twenty minutes later, Molly mentally goes over the discussion break-down that led to the Time-Out. She begins to think about her role and the things she could have done differently.

Mark: *"Molly, are you ready for a Time-In?"*

Molly: *"I think so."*

Mark: *"I was thinking about our conversation and I was out of line by launching into the money talk right away. I know our T-Time routine, and I skipped ahead to the business part right away. I could tell you were annoyed, but I plowed ahead anyway."*

Molly: *"I was surprised that you launched into the money talk right away. I could sense you were upset with the bill. I let my upset with your skipping the first part of our talk take over, and I gave you a few shots. I could have asked you if you were angry."*

Mark: *"I wasn't angry so much as frustrated and worried. I know this is a sensitive topic for you too, as I'm always bringing it up. I realize you're more relaxed about the dollars, and yet for some reason, I get really uptight. Maybe I'm just overly tired from work. I didn't sleep that well last night."*

Molly: *"I worry about our money as well, and want you to know that all the purchases were justified. I feel pressured sometimes when we talk about finances and feel I have to defend myself."*

Mark: *"I do come on a bit strong don't I? Why don't we leave this issue for now and hang out for awhile. We can discuss it later when we're both more rested and relaxed."*

Molly: *"Sounds great to me."*

RON AND ROSA

Ron and Rosa have worked through some mutual concerns and moved on to marriage. Rosa's fear of commitment has eased but she continues to be uneasy about communicating openly with Ron.

"Leave Me Alone!"

Ron: *"What do you want to do with all that old wood from the renovations?"*

Rosa: *"Let's get rid of it."*

Ron: *"I was thinking of cutting it up for firewood."*

Rosa: *"There's way too much! It will just rot."*

Ron: *"It seems like a waste to throw it away."*

Rosa: *(slightly irritated)* *"You never want to throw anything away."*

Ron: *(also slightly irritated)* *"There you go again about me being a pack rat."*

Rosa: *(frustrated)* *"Well what about all those boxes from your apartment you said you would go through and get rid of?"*

Ron: *(voice raised)* *"I told you I'd get to it. What have those boxes got to do with the wood? You're always bringing things up that aren't related to the topic at hand."*

Rosa: *(quietly)* *"I think they are related."*

Ron: *(annoyed)* *"I can't even ask a simple question without getting hassled.*

Rosa: *(Says nothing and leaves the room)*

Ron: *(voice more elevated)* *"Where are you going?"*

Rosa: *"I don't want to talk anymore."*

Ron: *(following Rosa with exasperation in his voice)* *"We're not finished yet!"*

Rosa: *(yelling)* *"Leave me alone!"*

WHAT *is happening here?*

Ron and Rosa have been doing well with their T-Times. Rosa is coming out of her shell more, and the results have been satisfying for both her and Ron. Instead of holding back her thoughts and feelings for fear of upsetting Ron, she has learned that opening up more helps her avoid getting depressed.

Rosa and Ron find it difficult to speak openly about certain topics. Actually, Ron is comfortable with such conversations, but Rosa finds it threatening. Ron, in turn, has trouble listening to Rosa when she's upset and withdrawn.

Rosa's parents fought a lot when she was a child and she hated it. She remembers putting her pillow over her head at night so that she wouldn't have to listen to them.

Ron doesn't understand what all the fuss is about. He likes to debate and enjoys finishing a topic when it comes up. It frustrates him that Rosa shuts down just when he's making some good points. Sometimes he follows her around the apartment trying to keep a discussion going after Rosa has said that she wants to stop.

TEAM TOOLS

Let's look at the Time-Out/Time-In strategy in greater detail.

Step One: Discuss the concept or strategy in advance and reach an agreement on whether to use it or not. A good time to raise the topic is during the "business" portion of the T-Time. This preliminary discussion explores the concept of Time-Out/Time-In to see how you both feel about it.

One of you, like Rosa, is likely to find the idea attractive. She has been trying to take breaks from discussions all the time, with limited success. She worries, however, that the Time-Out may not work.

Ron, on the other hand, doesn't like to leave things unfinished; therefore, he may not like the idea of taking a break. He believes, based on past experience, that Rosa won't return later (i.e. call a Time-In) to the topic at hand.

If you agree to use this strategy, it may be different from what you have tried to do in the past. First of all, it's important that you both agree in advance to use the technique. In the past, Rosa has tried to do something similar, but she didn't have Ron's agreement. This time, hopefully, she will.

Step Two: Once there is a willingness to use Time-Out/Time-In, the two of you need to agree on a way to call the break. Some couples use the words "Time-Out." Others find it better to make up some sort of personal code word or "non-verbal" sign to signal the Time-Out.

Willingness to use Time-Out will bolster Rosa's confidence in raising sensitive topics with Ron. She knows that if she starts to feel uncomfortable, she can call a break and Ron will respect it.

Step Three: Once a Time-Out is called, both partners immediately stop talking about the issue causing the problem.

It is crucial for the discussion of the sensitive issue to end. It is fine to move on to some other topic, or if strong feelings have been aroused, to stop talking altogether for a while.

Step Four: Settle down and think about your personal role in the deteriorating discussion.

At this stage, it's important not to take too long to calm down (i.e. several hours) and to think about the communication breakdown. One of you may want to get back to the discussion sooner than the other. If the Time-Out stretches on too long, this person will become frustrated.

If during Step Four you are unable to figure out anything you could have said or done differently, ask your spouse for input once you enter Step Five. (There is a good chance he or she will have several suggestions for you to consider!)

Step Five: Call for a Time-In only if both spouses agree.

Step Six: Start off the new discussion with observations about what you could have done differently (not what the other could have done).

It is suggested that one of you begin to talk about how you could have listened better than you did. Then the other one can do the same. Frequently, arguments begin because both parties in the conversation have stopped listening.

Beginning the Time-In with personal observations about your own behaviour is non-threatening to your mate. Beginning with observations about what the other could or should have done better (which is the usual way of returning to a topic) will probably lead to a renewed dispute.

Step Seven: Finish the original discussion.

As you return to the original discussion, you will both be listening more effectively because of the insights gained during the Time-Out. (This was covered in Chapter 7: "Consultation and Collaboration")

The discussion about different points of view begins with collaboration as the goal instead of the desire to win the other person over to your point of view. Sure, it can be fun to try to "win" the argument on occasion, but if the discussion doesn't seem to be working, it's important to change goals and "work the middle." You are trying to move from differing perspectives to a joint plan.

The same conversation with a Time-Out/Time-In:

Rosa: *(frustrated) "Well what about all those boxes from your apartment you said you would go through and get rid of?"*
Ron: *(voice raised) "I told you I'd get to it. What have those boxes got to do with the wood? You're always bringing things up that aren't related to the topic at hand."*
Rosa: *"Time-Out"*

After a cooling down period, either Ron or Rosa can take the initiative to call a Time-In. In this case, not surprisingly, Ron asked for a Time-In. He finds it hard not to complete a discussion once it starts.

Ron: *"Hi. Are you ready for a Time-In?"*
Rosa: *"No."*
Ron: *"Come on, it's been half an hour."*
Rosa: *"I'm still angry and not ready to talk about it."*
Ron: *(with frustration) "What's the sense of taking a Time-Out if you never get to do a Time-In?" (walks away in a huff.)*

WHAT is happening here?

In this case, Ron has cooled down and approached Rosa. She's not ready to return to the discussion, and Ron pushes. He gets frustrated right away, which may indicate that he wasn't as calm as he thought. If he approaches Rosa and she isn't ready, he needs to back off and give her more time.

For her part, Rosa knows that Ron likes to wrap up disagreements rather than leave them hanging, and she might try to speed up the process a little. In this case, she has been brooding about the argument rather than giving some thought to what she could have done differently or better. She's using the Time-Out to punish Ron.

TEAM TOOLS

Sometimes both spouses are ready to resume a conversation, but haven't quite followed the rules of Time-Out/Time-In.

Ron: *"Hi. Are you ready for a Time-In?"*
Rosa: *"Sure. Do you want to go first?"*
Ron: *"I don't care. You can go ahead if you like."*
Rosa: *"I don't think we would have had a hassle if you'd accepted my wish to get rid of the wood."*
Ron: *"Well it wasn't fair for you to bring in other issues. You love to do that."*

WHAT *is happening here?*

This Time-In isn't a Time-In at all, but a resumption of the argument. It is easy to take a Time-Out and ruminate on the mistakes or faults of the other. This can lead to the "Blame Game" (see "Definitions" in concluding chapter), where spouses focus completely on the faults of the other while ignoring their own. A power struggle can ensue and escalate dramatically in a destructive fashion.

TEAM TOOLS

When calling a Time-In, it's important to have taken enough time in the Time-Out for both parties to have cooled down. It is also crucial that each person "self-analyze and correct" the behaviour that led to the Time-Out. Only in this way will a constructive discussion take place with lessons learned, which may help to prevent a recurrence of this sort of argument.

Using Time-Out/Time-In:

Ron: *"Hi. Are you ready for a Time-In?"*
Rosa: *"I think so. Do you want me to start?"*
Ron: *"Sure, if you want to."*

Rosa: *"I don't think the talk we had was about the old wood at all. I was thinking about it and realized that I was still annoyed with you for not bringing home the plants I asked you to pick up. I said at the time I was fine, but I think I was actually more ticked off than I realized, and I should have said something. I know how you feel about wasting things and I agree that it's good to recycle things instead of throwing them away. I guess I'm also bothered about the boxes that never get moved. In spite of this frustration, I didn't have to accuse you of things and make a big issue out of it.*

Ron: *"I was surprised that our talk about the wood took off as it did. I seemed to hit a nerve with you, and I didn't stop to ask you what it was. I could sense there was something more going on, but I got caught up in the issue instead of your feelings. I keep forgetting to check in with your* *feelings when they show up. Old habits die hard it seems.*

"Let's list the Tips..."

• Calling a Time-out prevents a power struggle.

• Learning from our mistakes enriches a relationship.

• Call a Time-In when both of you are ready to do so.

• Self correction is the key to a good Time-In.

• Time-out/Time-in prevents recurring arguments.

CHAPTER NINE

Forgive Frequently

Any two people trying to make a life together are going to irritate or unintentionally hurt each other from time to time. Strong marriages are made up of regular people who occasionally get under each other's skin.

These couples have their rough moments, but are able to bounce back quickly because of the following skills and habits:

- Good attitudes
- Talking regularly
- Listening effectively
- Working as a team
- Taking time to have fun regularly
- Most important, being merciful

Little has been written in psychological literature about forgiveness. Recently, a few books have appeared, and for the most part they are excellent.

One author states that one shouldn't forgive another person "unless they have asked for it." She says that if a person has hurt us and didn't apologize, or died before he could, he can't be forgiven for what he said or did. The problem with this approach to forgiveness is that it gives a lot of power to the person who causes pain.

It is emotionally liberating to forgive another person. Someone who has experienced the death of a loved one and who hasn't let go of their interpersonal issues with them may not be able to fully grieve until they do so. Unhealthy or complicated grief reactions arise, such as being stuck in one emotion, or having prolonged and increasingly intense reactions. In both cases there is "unfinished business," and until it is finished, the grief won't heal.

Letting go of a deceased person may require a letter in which negative and positive memories are shared. At the end of the letter there needs to be forgiveness so that the letting go can be accomplished. If there is no forgiveness, the pain regenerates, often more intensely than the original hurt.

Not to forgive unless one is asked to do so may leave one stuck in one's woundedness. Christian teachings have been clear that frequent forgiveness is not negotiable, but rather a requirement of faith. Believers and non-believers alike would be wise to heed this teaching, as it is excellent psychology.

Early in my marriage, a friend gave me some advice. He told me to start each day fresh. To do this, it would be necessary to let go of the issues from the day before and see my wife with "new eyes." When I've followed this wisdom, I have been able to move beyond grudges and left-over annoyances. Such an attitude hasn't prevented us from examining and resolving differences, but rather, aids the process by clearing out the animosity.

In the "Peace with the Past" chapter (Chapter 2), there were many examples of couples exploring their history to learn about themselves and their sensitivities. Inherent in these stories was forgiveness. The secret to making "peace" is the ability to see things objectively and to let go of old hurts.

NIGEL

Introduction: Nigel is a young widower who is angry about a failed relationship.

Anger Gets in the Way

Nigel's wife died a few years before we met, and he assured me that he was coping well with her death. He had recently been dating someone with whom he'd fallen in love almost at first sight. The problem was, the new love "dumped" Nigel, and he was now very upset. In fact, he was furi-

ous with her, and had trouble getting past the anger so as to move on. I suggested that he'd have to forgive her if he wanted to move on. He snapped back that he was "too angry to forgive her."

WHAT is happening here?

The interesting sideline to this story is that Nigel had never been "dumped" in his life. He was insulted and annoyed that this new love interest could be so brazen as to dump him—of all people! The novelty of the experience was part of the difficulty in moving on, but there was more going on there as well.

TEAM TOOLS

When we experience a loss, it's important to share the pain related to the loss. This sharing can be done through conversation and/or writing, and will help to ease the upset. Once the emotions have settled somewhat, it's easier to forgive and move on. Such a step won't eliminate the return of the emotions, but when they return, they will be less intense each time.

Learning to forgive:

Nigel realized that he was too angry with his ex-girlfriend to forgive her for dumping him. It occurred to both of us that the intensity of his anger was extreme, and perhaps not just related to the jilting experience.

We returned to his wife and her illness and death. Nigel began to weep and expressed surprise that he was so upset, as he thought he'd moved on from this tragic loss. He realized that he was also angry with his wife for dying. He then expressed guilt at feeling this way.

Nigel was able to write his wife a letter and tell her how much her love meant to him, and how angry he felt at her leaving him. He then forgave her for dying. Afterwards, we returned to his recent dating experience and he was surprised that he felt much less upset about this loss. He let it go and moved on.

TIP: Feel first and then forgive.

Does It Mean It Was OK?

Following a speech I gave about relationships and marriage to a group of high school students, a young woman approached me. She said that she had trouble with forgiveness. Her boyfriend had been unfaithful to her and she thought that if she forgave him it would mean that what he did was okay.

WHAT is happening here?

Because so little has been written and taught about forgiveness outside of religious circles, there are misperceptions about what it means to take this step. This young woman would be unable to forgive her boyfriend because she thought it meant that his actions were acceptable. By not forgiving him, however, she would actually hurt herself more than him.

TEAM TOOLS

Forgiveness doesn't mean that what happened to cause the pain was acceptable. It wasn't. Forgiveness is about preventing the wounded person from continuing to hurt. The perpetrator may not care one way or the other.

This young woman seemed to think that if she forgave her boyfriend his indiscretion, she would have to stay in the relationship. She could stay or move on, but would be free from carrying a grudge that would probably interfere with her committing to any new relationship.

Learning to forgive:

This young woman realized that she could forgive and still end the relationship. (She could also have chosen to stay in the relationship, and it wouldn't have meant that what her boyfriend had done was acceptable.) By forgiving, she will be in better shape to have a new relationship down the road.

TIP: Forgiveness doesn't make what happened acceptable.

VERONICA AND VINCE

A bankruptcy has added stress to this couple's relationship and made it harder for Veronica to trust Vince and the changes he has made.

Afraid to Forgive

Veronica and Vince have worked hard to improve their marriage after a brief separation and bankruptcy trauma, but in spite of this effort, there is ongoing suspicion (sometimes this can happen because there is worry about being hurt again). The T-Times are working well for them, and trust is rebuilding, but they seem to have hit a wall.

WHAT is happening here?

There are times when a couple work hard and build their bond, but there is still tension or suspicion. Time and ongoing communication will help to rebuild trust. (see Chapter 10 - After the Crisis the Rebuild)

TEAM TOOLS

If a couple have decided to move ahead in their marriage after a crisis, and healing still fails to occur, it may be related to an underlying fear. Just like a couple who are afraid to commit and will avoid going deeper in their relationship, sometimes the wounded spouse is afraid to let her guard down, and thereby risk further hurt. In this case, forgiveness can be held back as a protection from further hurt.

Learning to forgive:

Vince and Veronica are doing their talks and walks and have been collaborating better than ever. In spite of all this good effort, Veronica remains somewhat aloof, and at times, suspicious of Vince. He tries to be patient but is getting frustrated, and his upset feeds into Veronica's worry about being hurt again by his lack of consultation.

At a certain point, Veronica is able to talk about her fear of being wounded again, and she says she's not letting go of her old hurt for this reason. This discussion helps her to realize what impact her fear is having on the rebuilding of the marriage, and she is able to let go and finally forgive.

TIP: **Fear can get in the way of forgiveness.**

RON AND ROSA

The changes this couple have made have rippled out to their extended families. Ron has also learned that he needs to give feedback when he listens and that a break can sometimes ease tension and improve listening.

Forgive and Forget?

Rosa's father died when she was young. She has now returned to that loss and discussed it in detail. She also wrote a letter to her father and forgave him for dying and abandoning her. In spite of this good effort and the resulting deepened commitment with her husband and other family members, Rosa is worried, as she has heard that it's necessary to "forgive and forget"

WHAT is happening here?

Rosa has done well in revisiting her past and exploring her old pain related to the suppressed grief about her father's death. Her lingering upset is caused by friends telling her that she has to forget about her father's death as part of moving on.

> **TEAM TOOLS**
>
> Forgiving and forgetting have been linked for a good reason. The point may be that if you don't forgive, you won't be able to forget. On the other hand, if you do forgive, it doesn't mean that forgetting is necessarily part of the process. Rosa doesn't want to forget about her father's premature death. Such memories are part of her connection with her father, and aren't

■ getting in the way of her being close to her husband and family.

Learning to forgive:

Rosa has let go of her resentment towards her father for dying so young. She doesn't forget her father though, as she values the few faint memories she has of her time with him. She also recalls the hurt and loneliness she felt, and in some way, these feelings have become part of her ongoing connection with her father. She is now able to get close to others, as she has let her father go through the act of forgiveness.

TIP: It is OK to forgive and not forget.

STAN AND SUSAN

Stan has learned that Susan may be listening well and disagreeing with him at the same time.

Skeletons in the Closet

Stan and Susan have done well in the rebuilding of their marriage. Susan has made changes, which pleases Stan, and he's done the same for her.

Stan has forgiven Susan, but from time to time he recalls some incident from the past, and he's annoyed all over again. Susan has been patient with these memories, and asked him if he has really forgiven her.

WHAT is happening here?

Stan has let go of his old resentments related to Susan's aggressive debating style, but he continues to feel some resentment at times. It's not surprising that Susan has questioned Stan's degree of forgiveness.

TEAM TOOLS

Just because forgiveness has been offered, it doesn't mean that there is forgetting, as mentioned above. Sometimes the memories have an emotional aspect that needs attention. An upsetting event can occur, and an apology can be offered and accepted, but if the feelings related to the event aren't well heard, they can linger. When Stan is angry in the present moment, he may bring up old issues that are now corrected, and this would indicate that there's some old emotion to be explored.

Learning to forgive:

Stan and Susan are dealing with a money matter, and Stan becomes frustrated and annoyed. Susan acknowledges his upset before making her point less aggressively, in hopes of achieving collaboration. Stan brings up the "old days" when Susan took care of the money herself and when he didn't feel comfortable giving his opinions.

Stan: *"You always take over with the money!"*
Susan: *"That was a long time ago. I thought we're doing better now."*
Stan: *"Well we are, but sometimes it seems you're taking over again."*
Susan: *"Are you angry with my current thoughts on the budget?"*
Stan: *"I guess I'm frustrated that you don't like my great idea."*
Susan: *"There's something more though, something bigger than that. Are you still feeling angry about things that happened between us in the past, even though we've made some good changes?"*
Stan: *"Yes, I think I am. It surprises me that some of the old memories carry such a punch, even now."*
Susan: *"Tell me more..."*

TIP: Old memories may still have feelings attached.

MOLLY AND MARK

This couple have discovered that a periodic time-out can help them to deal with sensitive topics more effectively.

Birth of the Blame Game

Mel has a tendency to blame Molly for problems or differences of opinion they experience when they are planning for a trip, or even day-to-day activities. Mel will sometimes blame Molly in public as well. She has expressed frustration that he's always making things "her fault."

WHAT is happening here?

When he's frustrated, Mel has a tendency to look for someone to blame. He seems to do this automatically, in spite of showing some signs of improving. Mel is surprised when Molly accuses him of "always blaming her," although he has noticed the tendency himself and isn't sure why it happens.

TEAM TOOLS

When a person automatically blames others for problems rather than looking at himself and taking some responsibility as well, it may indicate that there's some old issue that hasn't been forgiven. When forgiveness is withheld, it makes it difficult, if not impossible, to forgive in the present. A tendency such as blaming may also indicate emotional immaturity connected to some incidents that took place in the past that were not well debriefed.

Learning to forgive:

Molly still thinks that Mel verbally attacks her and blames her for incidents beyond her control. Mel is concerned about his behaviour as well. He acknowledges that when he's frustrated, the first thought that comes to his mind is "What did you do now Molly?" In one instance, he had misplaced his shoes and wondered out loud what Molly had done with them.

At that point, he realized that he was blaming her for things that she had nothing to do with. Mel decided to do some research. He brought out his journal and began to write some memories related to growing up with his birth family. He recalled some incidents in his teens when his father had been particularly strict. He hadn't been able to share his resulting upset, as his father wouldn't hear of it. As he wrote, some of the old feelings began to surface, and Mel was surprised at how strong they were.

He realized, in tears, that he hadn't forgiven his father for being such a strict disciplinarian. This insight led to some strong upset, as Mel's father had died, and Mel hadn't grieved openly until that moment. Mel shared his writing with Molly and she offered her support. Both Mel and Molly noticed that Mel was no longer a master "blame game" player in the weeks that followed.

TIP: Forgiveness helps to stop the Blame Game.

"Let's review the Tips..."

• Feel first and then forgive.

• Forgiveness doesn't make what happened acceptable.

• Fear can get in the way of forgiveness.

• Old memories may still have feelings attached.

• Forgiveness helps to stop the Blame Game.

After The Crisis - The Rebuild

REBUILD - A marriage that could become a "low conflict divorce" if something isn't done to repair it. This relationship has broken down or slipped into crisis and can't continue as it once was. Changes need to be made to revitalize the relationship.

This chapter is an "add-on" to the original concept of this book. It is offered as an aid to those couples who have survived an affair or flat marriage syndrome, and decided to rebuild their marriage.

During the rebuilding process, which can take several months, there are concerns that can arise from either spouse. These concerns can add tension to an already stressful situation, and can lead to a derailment of the rebuilding process.

What follows are some typical issues that can arise during a rebuild process.

FRANK AND FELICITY

Felicity and Frank separated due to differences in philosophy and Frank's affair. After a period apart, Frank ends his extra marital relationship and approaches Felicity to rebuild the marriage. She cautiously agrees to try.

Cool the Jets

Felicity had received the shock of her life when she discovered that Frank had been secretly having an affair. Frank has decided to leave his outside relationship, but Felicity isn't sure she will take him back. Frank is scared

and is working overtime to make things good for Felicity. He's very af-
fectionate and accommodating, but Felicity says that she's uncomfortable
because of the pressure of Frank's "trying too hard." Frank is frustrated
with Felicity's guardedness. The harder he tries, the more she withdraws.

WHAT is happening here?

This couple are in the process of redefining their marriage. Because of
his fear, Frank is going flat out to make things better for Felicity, but
he's overwhelming her at the same time. Felicity is feeling pressured
and isn't picking up on Frank's worry.

TEAM TOOLS

When a spouse receives a "wake-up call" from a crisis, he can
panic and try too hard to make things better. His wife will
welcome the effort for the most part, but may feel uncomfortable at the same time. So much change in a short time can lead
to the spouse feeling three things: 1. pleased to see the change,
2. somewhat angry that so much is happening all of a sudden
when things were poor for so long, and 3. a certain lack of
trust that the changes will stick.

Rebuilding after the crisis:

Felicity asks Frank if he's fearful that they may not be able to rebuild
their marriage, and he says he is. They have come so close to letting go of
the marriage. Felicity tells him she's overwhelmed by his changes and
would prefer if he backed off a little. Frank wasn't aware of his negative
impact on Felicity, and thanks her for the feedback.

TIP: *Too much change, too fast, backfires!*

The Fog Bank

Some time has passed and Frank is asking Felicity how she's feeling
about the marriage. She is warming up, but isn't completely sure that
she's back in the marriage for good. Frank is frustrated, as he finds the
uncertainty difficult.

WHAT *is happening here?*

This couple is making good progress, but Frank is still worried. He's not sure where this rebuilding is really headed, and it worries him that they may not be the happy couple he envisions. He's trying to look into the future and can't yet get a reading.

> **TEAM TOOLS**
>
> During the rebuilding process, it can be difficult for one or both spouses to allow some time to pass. Changes need to unfold over time, sometimes several months, until the new relationship is sustained. Trying to see the future during the rebuilding process can be like trying to see the horizon in a fog bank. When surrounded by fog, each person needs to take things one step at a time. Trying to rush things will only lead to frustration. Accepting the environment as it is can even lead to happiness with one's immediate life and surroundings.

Rebuilding after the crisis:

Felicity and Frank have been rebuilding for about six weeks. Frank has been pacing himself, and instead of doing things that overwhelm Felicity, he has been speaking about his fears. Felicity has been able to share some of her anger and worry as well. Both are struggling with trust issues. Frank has stopped thinking about the distant future or wanting assurances from Felicity. The result is that the relationship is mending and warming up slowly but surely, and both Felicity and Frank are encouraged.

TIP: In the Rebuild (fog), move ahead carefully, one step at a time.

Flashback

This couple are becoming more confident about their rebuild. Then Felicity begins to think about the old relationship and how she felt. These memories discourage her, and she's distant when she returns home that evening.

WHAT *is happening here?*

It is not uncommon for the betrayed spouse to be cautious about re-engaging during a marital rebuild. It takes time for confidence to build in the new patterns of communication and collaboration. It can set things back when the spouse recalls the "bad old days" and worries that they will return.

TEAM TOOLS

Trusting that changes will last takes time and patience from both spouses. It's not unusual to recall the difficult times; for the unhappy spouse, these memories can be scary. When a couple are faced with a deteriorating relationship, there are only two options open to them: improve the relationship or end it. If the future isn't much better than the past, the couple will likely divorce.

Rebuilding after the crisis:

Felicity is discouraged and quiet, and Frank is immediately uneasy. During their T-Time, Frank reaches out and Felicity is able to tell him about her worry. He tells her that he doesn't want to go back to the old ways. He admits that he likes the changes they're making, and that life is better than it ever was.

TIP: A *successful rebuilt marriage is stronger and healthier than the old relationship.*

VINCE AND VERONICA

This couple separated briefly, as Veronica had reached the point where she was no longer willing to appease Vince. She was very angry and wasn't really open to trying to do a rebuild.

The following sequence of scenarios relates back to the struggles of Vince and Veronica trying to rebuild their relationship.

Commit To See if One Is Able to Commit

Vince has had his "wake-up call" and Veronica is acting as if she's finished with the marriage. She's angrier than ever, and she's also tired of the old routines of appeasing Vince. He has reacted in shock and fear and wants to go for counselling, which Veronica does reluctantly. She tells the psychologist that she's fed up and doesn't think she can recommit to the marriage.

WHAT *is happening here?*

When a spouse appeases over time, there may come a point where she can no longer do so. It's as if a pendulum has swung and the appeaser moves from one extreme to the other. In the process, this person can lose hope that things will improve.

TEAM TOOLS

When the pendulum swings for an accommodating spouse, it can signal the end of the marriage. This type of personality doesn't like conflict, and will hang on until she can no longer, believing the marriage is over.

The other spouse is upset and wants the discouraged mate to commit to going ahead in the marriage. This may be difficult for her to do. It's enough to commit to doing some work to see if the marriage can be saved. Usually this is a workable approach, particularly if there are children involved. In this situation, the couple need to parent together for the rest of their lives, whether they stay together or not.

Rebuilding after the crisis:

Veronica is very angry and tells the marriage therapist that she's tired of trying to make her marriage work. Vince, in his worry for the relationship, is asking her to commit to a rebuild, but Veronica is unwilling to do so. The psychologist asks her to commit to improving the relationship as a friendship, with no talk of ongoing marriage. Because of the children, Veronica is willing to engage in some level of rebuilding. Over time, the progress is encouraging to both Vince and Veronica, and they move on to a full scale rebuild of the marriage.

TIP: **Commit to trying to commit.**

Settle Down Sexually

Vince has been buzzing around Veronica, trying to make things better. Part of his new attentiveness involves saying multiple "I love you" statements and offering numerous hugs. Veronica rejects his invitations for physical intimacy, and asks Vince to stop telling her he loves her.

WHAT is happening here?

As mentioned with Frank and Felicity above, it's not uncommon for the shocked spouse to try hard to do everything possible to salvage the marriage. Often these attempts can include invitations to resume sexual contact. I recall the first clients I ever worked with. The husband told me that their sex life was poor, and if I could help them fix it, everything would be fine.

It turned out that the wife had shut down, saying that it was impossible for her to be sexually intimate when her husband worked out of town a lot. They rarely spoke with each other, and therefore, she didn't feel an emotional connection.

TEAM TOOLS

When the sexual aspect of the relationship has disappeared, it can be missed by one spouse more than the other. I used to think it was related to gender, but it seems that it has to do more with personality than gender; I've met both men and women who shut down sexually when the emotional bond is weak.

A spouse who pushes for sex in hopes of warming up his mate is likely projecting his own need for closeness on his wife. He would feel less fearful if they could interact in this way, and yet the more he pushes, the more distant his wife becomes.

Rebuilding after the crisis:

Vince expresses his frustration with the lack of sexual intimacy, which Veronica accepts and understands. She expresses relief that Vince is willing to back off until they are further along in their rebuild.

Veronica: *"I'm not interested in sex right now. I wish you would back off!"*
Vince: *"OK, OK, I thought that getting close might help."*
Veronica: *"I know you mean well, but I have to feel closer to you first."*
Vince: *"I've been worried that you may not warm up, and we'll be done."*
Veronica: *"I think it's getting better between us."*
Vince: *"I get frustrated when we aren't intimate. I miss you."*
Veronica: *"I miss you too, but it takes time. Thanks for backing off."*

TIP: Talking and good listening can be early stage lovemaking.

The Warming Trend

Vince and Veronica are doing their T-Times and collaborating better than ever. Both of them are feeling encouraged, but Vince has noticed that Veronica is still physically distant. Vince tells her that it's really starting to bother him that she's so "cold."

WHAT is happening here?

In spite of some good effort and the passage of time, the physical intimacy has not returned for this couple. Vince has backed off in the hope that things will warm up, but after a period of time, he sees no change. He begins to express his upset, and Veronica feels attacked.

TEAM TOOLS

During the rebuilding process, it can seem to take an eternity for the sexual part of the relationship to return. It probably took some time for the sexual closeness to shut down, so it takes time for it to resume (although not as long as it took to disappear).

It's not like flicking a switch so much as a gradual warming trend, which eventually leads to renewed intimacy. Some spouses won't even be open to touching or hugs, as they worry that this will be misread as an invitation for more intimacy, which they aren't ready for yet.

Rebuilding after the crisis:

In therapy, Vince expresses his frustration with the lack of sex. The therapist asks Veronica if she is as shut down sexually as she was a few months ago, and she says "No." He draws a line on a white board with the old marriage noted on the left and the new marriage on the far right, with a line between. He points out to Vince that they were previously at the far left.

The therapist asks Veronica where she is on the line between the two extremes, and she points to a spot about mid way between the two. Vince is encouraged to see that there is a warming trend, and this gives him hope.

Veronica has said that she isn't comfortable with hugs, as they often lead to Vince trying to "go the distance." This means that there is no cuddling or touching, and this lack of contact accentuates the distance between them. A deal is worked out where Vince will ask Veronica if she would be open to a hug, and he won't take it further. This collaboration takes pressure off both of them and helps to speed up the warming trend.

TIP: Renewed sexual intimacy warms up gradually over time.

Suspicion

Time has passed, and Veronica and Vince are doing much better. The pain caused by the bankruptcy has settled, and there is a good level of communication and collaboration. In spite of the progress, Veronica periodically becomes suspicious of Vince and will accuse him of not being completely open with her about their finances. Vince finds these accusa-

tions offensive and scary, as he thinks he may have to put up with these suspicions for the rest of his life.

WHAT is *happening here*?

When trust has been violated by an affair or deterioration in a relationship, it can take some time to mend (months, not years). T-Times help immensely to rebuild trust. This couple is doing well, but the suspicions continue to linger. Veronica is upset with her fears, as she believes that she and Vince are doing well; she isn't sure why she feels this way.

TEAM TOOLS

The good news about rebuilding trust is that it can and will grow if the proper steps are taken. T-Times with compassionate listening and good collaboration will help immensely. In spite of these steps, suspicions can sometimes linger.

When a marriage suffers a trauma, that experience leaves its imprint within one or both spouses. In the future, when stresses accumulate, they can seem like an echo of the original trauma. With some good listening, it becomes clear right away that what first appears as suspicion is really fatigue or worry about a child or other concerns.

This couple is learning that when suspicion arises, it's usually the tip of an iceberg, with other feelings close by. For a time, any worry or concern may show up as suspicion.

Rebuilding after the crisis:

Veronica is happy with the progress that she and Vince have been making. From time to time, suspicions arise around money matters. She is surprised when this happens, as they've been doing very well.

When Veronica voices her concerns, it's hard for Vince to hear her without getting defensive. He knows that feelings tend to "travel in packs," and so he asks what else might be happening. The suspicious thoughts and feelings break away, and other issues of concern surface and are discussed. Both Vince and Veronica are trying to be patient with Veronica's suspicious feelings.

TIP: Rebuilding trust takes time.

"Let's review the Tips..."

• Too much change, too fast, backfires!

• In the Rebuild (fog), move ahead carefully, one step at a time.

• A successful rebuilt marriage is stronger and healthier than the old relationship.

• Commit to trying to commit.

• Talking and good listening can be early stage lovemaking.

• Renewed sexual intimacy warms up gradually over time.

• Rebuilding trust takes time.

Chapter Eleven

Laugh, Play & Encourage

Laugh a lot

"Laugh....and reap the benefits!" This appropriate line is taken from the book Head First - The Biology of Hope, in which author Norman Cousins notes that when we laugh, we exercise our internal organs, and release endorphins at the same time.

A shared sense of humour can lighten the struggles of everyday life. It feels good to end each T-Time session on a light note by recalling something positive about the day, complimenting one another, or sharing a joke.

A sense of humour can be invaluable in repairing a troubled marriage. I have noticed over the years that when a couple shares a sense of humour, they are more likely to be successful in therapy. Humour helps everyone involved to lighten up and not take themselves too seriously.

A colleague of mine has a wonderful sense of humour. When he shares a joke or a funny story, his wife laughs first and loudest. She thinks he's hysterical, and yet she's heard his stories countless times before. Couples who enjoy each other's humour usually have a strong bond.

TIP: *Life is too important to be taken seriously*!

Play or Date

During courtship, we spend a lot of time and energy enjoying each other and ourselves. Once a commitment is made and other responsibilities follow (particularly children), it's too easy to stop having fun. Single people or couples without children enjoy leisure time in a variety of ways. Married couples with children would also benefit from getting out together and having a life apart from their parental roles. To enhance the relationship, it's important for a couple to date and "play" regularly as a twosome.

Play times tend to naturally grow out of T-Times. When a couple is dating before marriage, there is a willingness to participate in activities the other enjoys. Often, this willingness to be adventurous wanes with marriage, and each spouse slips into the mindset of doing what they enjoy doing and discounting the priorities of the other.

We have seen from earlier examples that it can be beneficial for each person to stretch into the interests of the other. The important thing is for the couple to spend time together; the method they use is secondary. Here is a flashback to the Attitude chapter:

TEAM TOOLS

When a couple has a chance to do something together, it's irrelevant which activity they choose. In fact, because of different interests, it may be impossible to find a shared activity. The main goal is to spend time together and make the relationship the focus, even if the activity isn't the first choice of one of the spouses.

When a married person makes it a priority to have fun **outside** the marriage, it's usually a sign that the relationship is weak or soon will be.

TIP: *Dates or playtimes help to keep the fun in a marriage*

Encourage

It's good for spouses to acknowledge their love regularly. It is particularly wise to remind each other of this love when the consultation/collaboration process breaks down.

When it comes to acknowledging our love, there are two important points. First of all, each partner needs to find out how the other likes to be loved. Secondly, each one has to be open to the other person's own particular way of showing love. Often we love each other the way we want to be loved, or the way we saw our parents or others love each other when we were growing up.

Put simply, each one will do well by discovering and meeting the "needs" of the other. Each partner can make a list of what makes them happy, and then discuss the lists with each other. This would help each partner to be more aware of the other's preferences. One spouse may like hugs and want them from a partner who isn't a big hugger, but who does chores well. The hugger could see love in the other person's effort to do chores immediately and effectively. On the other hand, the non-hugger could offer some hugs or share more affection with their partner because she values such interaction.

TIP: *Love your spouse the way she/he wants to be loved.*

BETH AND BOB

Bob and Beth are settling into their new marriage. Bob is the talker, but he has been selective at times in what he shares. Beth is opening up more with Bob, and they are getting better at collaborating when they have their individual plans.

Laugh With Me, Not At Me

Bob and Beth are socializing with some old friends. Beth becomes quiet at a certain point in the conversation, as a friend has said something to upset her. Bob notices that Beth has withdrawn, and jokes about her "shutting down again." He's trying to lighten things up.

WHAT *is happening here?*

Bob and Beth have been learning more about each other as they move ahead in their marriage. Bob knows that Beth can be introverted at times, and it worries and bothers him. He wants to help, but his frustration colours the effort, and he ends up putting Beth down with his joking about her quietness.

TEAM TOOLS

It can be a challenge not to react with discomfort when a spouse is doing something we think they should change. The result is that everyone begins to feel awkward and uncomfortable. Humour can indeed lighten things up, but it can also be a means of criticism. (Sarcasm is an example of negative humour.) Here's a situation where some supportive statement might have been more helpful.

Let's revisit the above story and see how Bob's support could have changed the outcome.

Beth becomes quiet during a conversation with old friends. Bob picks up on her silence and touches her hand. He asks her how she's doing. Beth says that she's fine and tells him that she has been reminded of an old hurt by something mentioned in the conversation. She goes on to describe her memory and concern, and almost immediately feels better. The general conversation resumes.

TIP: Support is better than sarcasm

Laugh With Me

Bob and Beth are talking about their plans for the weekend and Bob goes on at some length about what he has in mind for them. At a certain point he realizes he's forgetting to ask Beth what her thoughts and plans were, as they had originally planned to spend part of Saturday doing chores together. He pauses and asks Beth what's on her agenda.

WHAT is happening here?

This couple is attempting to consult about their weekend activities and Bob gets carried away in outlining his plans, which is easy enough to do. He is able to catch himself, however, and this allows Beth a chance to join the conversation. Had he gone on, Beth may have become upset and withdrawn, or said something critical.

TEAM TOOLS

When a person is trying to change certain behaviours, insight isn't enough. It can take time and practice to do things differently. Bob is able to catch himself and he quietly adjusts what he's doing, which is great. However, he misses a chance to laugh at himself and his tendency to dominate the planning process. Such humour would be well received and pull Beth into the discussion quickly.

Let's continue with the same conversation:

Bob then adds "There I go again, rambling on with all my important plans. I'm good at that aren't I?" He laughs, and Beth smiles in return. She then offers some of her priorities and they go on to make a joint plan.

TIP: Laugh at your foibles.

GORD AND GINA

In addition to making time for talks and collaboration, Gord and Gina have decided to do more together as a couple.

Date Night

Gord and Gina have been doing their T-Times with increasing success, and Gina is more assertive than in the past. After their talks, they dive into household or yard chores or crash on the couch and watch TV. Generally, they are busy doing solo projects, which take up most evenings including weekends.

WHAT is happening here?

Many couples live busy lives involving themselves in personal projects at home or in the community. In doing so, they minimize the time they have together. This couple is doing well because they make time for T-Times most days. (Some marriage counsellors suggest date nights as a tool to help fix a troubled marriage, but if there are not regular

T-Times, this suggestion won't bear fruit.)

TEAM TOOLS

Busy lives can lead to very little time spent together as a couple. Making the T-Times a reality is a good first step, but it's important to have fun together as well. Dating without "talks" will usually fall flat; however, talks with dating can work well.

Recently, Gord and Gina have felt the need to spend more quality time together and have decided to schedule a regular date night. They often go to a movie (each one takes a turn choosing the film), and at times, they add in a dinner as well. They have noticed that they talk even more freely and effectively during these outings and are laughing more as well.

TIP: **Talks and dates make a good combination.**

JOHN AND JOAN

John and Joan have come a long way in their relationship and are moving ahead nicely in their new marriage. John continues to struggle with opening up, and Joan is trying not to pressure him too much.

Love the other...

John and Joan have been married for over a year and have been doing well in many ways. They decide, however, to visit their psychologist for a "check-up." Joan is frustrated that John isn't more openly affectionate. He claims that it's not his style to say "I love you" regularly; besides, Joan should know he loves her because he does almost everything she asks. If, for instance, she wants a picture hung, he hangs it!

WHAT *is happening here?*

This couple has different ways of showing affection, and this isn't unusual. John is not openly affectionate with his words, but rather, "shows" his love by doing chores on demand for Joan. She appreciates John's cooperation, but she's a romantic and likes to have feedback and kind words. At times she wonders if John really loves her when he doesn't express his love with words.

TEAM TOOLS

It's not unusual for spouses to express affection in different ways. This is normal and healthy, although challenging as well. The Golden Rule states "love another as you would like to be loved," and this can be taken literally.

It may be best to ask the other person "how" he or she would like to be loved, and go from there. The result is that each spouse reaches out in an unaccustomed way and learns through the process.

Your Turn...

(Cover the section below and write on a note pad how you might resolve this issue.)

Joan and John's therapist suggested that they "Love their spouse the way their spouse wants to be loved," and they have both taken the idea to heart. John has never been good at saying "I love you" or offering praise, but he's been making attempts to do both. He has even managed to write a few love notes to Joan.

For her part, Joan is noticing when John does things for her, and is thanking him more than she used to. She recognizes John's hands-on approach to love when he does chores or special projects around their home.

TIP: **Be open to showing love in new ways.**

MARK AND MOLLY

Mark is much more open than he was in the past, but at times, is perhaps too forthcoming. He will now criticize Molly in front of their friends, which is something he wouldn't have done in the past.

United We Stand

Mark and Molly have some friends over for dinner. At a certain point Mark comments that they could have been eating by now, but Molly is running late. Molly ignores this remark and keeps stirring a pot on the stove.

WHAT *is happening here?*

Mark is frustrated about dinner being late and makes a negative comment to his wife in front of their friends. His attempt to assuage his friends ends up shaming Molly. She keeps her upset to herself in spite of the awkward silence that follows Mark's comment.

TEAM TOOLS

Critical comments are best made privately, if at all, so that no one is embarrassed or upset. If an explanation is necessary, it can be given without injuring the other spouse. Explaining a delay to friends is fine, but not in a way that hurts the other person.

Your Turn...

(Cover the section below and write on a note pad how you might resolve this issue.)

Mark says that they would have been on time if he had helped Molly earlier. He jokes that he was very busy watching the football game instead. Molly smiles along with the friends and nods her head in agreement.

TIP: *Praise in public is great; criticism is not!*

OLIVIA AND OSSIE

Ossie and Oliva have always been good at embracing each other's tastes, but when it comes to offering support in times of trouble their personal styles get in the way. However, they are generally communicating better than they once did, with less reactive behaviour.

Space or No Space

Ossie is a hugger and Olivia is not. When he's upset, he likes to have some hands-on comfort. When Olivia is upset, she likes space. Olivia's father has died and she is very upset. She has withdrawn, and Ossie is hugging her in an attempt to comfort her. Olivia isn't responding, and Ossie is becoming frustrated and worried.

WHAT *is happening here?*

During an upsetting time, it's natural to reach out to a loved one, and Ossie is doing his best to comfort Olivia. He is reaching out in the way he's most comfortable and, coincidentally, the way he prefers for himself. In this situation, it isn't having the desired impact and Ossie is distressed.

TEAM TOOLS

It is common to reach out to others in the way we like to be supported ourselves. It may seem that this approach isn't working when the other person is looking for some other style of comfort. In marriage, it can be very helpful to the relationship if each partner does a little homework and observes the preferences of the other, and then tailors the gesture of love to meet the expectations of the other person.

Ossie thinks about Olivia's reaction and puts aside his own feelings of helplessness. He tells her that he's there for her, but is going to give her space as long as she needs it. He will check back with her to see how she's doing later.

TIP: Be aware of your spouse's emotional needs.

Hugs Help

Ossie has been struggling with a challenge at work and it has left him very frustrated. He has been sharing his concern with Olivia, and reaches a point where he's in tears. Olivia can see his upset and decides to give him some privacy. Ossie becomes annoyed and asks her why she's leaving.

WHAT is happening here?

Olivia enjoys time to herself, particularly if she's tearful. She has assumed that this is a good way to support Ossie when he's in tears. She knows he's a hugger, but at this upsetting moment, she has reached out in the way she prefers to be treated herself. She hasn't thought that it might be appropriate to offer Ossie a hug.

> ### TEAM TOOLS
>
> Even when a spouse realizes that her mate has different ways of sharing affection, it may not occur to her to "do what he does." It can be a creative gesture of love to observe the spouse and offer him what he seems to value. The challenge here is that the spouse offering the support may be doing something that she finds uncomfortable, i.e. giving a hug or giving space when she is not accustomed to doing so.

Your Turn...

(Cover the section below and write on a note pad how you might resolve this issue.)

The same situation with a different response:

While talking about a work-related problem, Ossie begins to weep. Olivia has been listening and offers Ossie a tissue. She touches his arm and asks him if he'd like a hug. He nods his head, and they share a long embrace. Afterwards, Ossie thanks Olivia for her support.

TIP: Love is creative.

STAN AND SUSAN

Stan and Susan have been rebuilding their marriage after a separation, and are doing well. Listening still remains a challenge for them, but they are seeing improvements.

Giving What I Want

Stan and Susan are visiting Stan's parents, as it is Stan's father's birthday. Stan has bought a beer mug for his dad. It is metal with a glass bottom and has a deer horn handle. He's sure his father will like the gift. However, over the next few months, Stan notices that the mug is on a shelf in the dining room where other knick-knacks are stored by his mother.

WHAT *is happening here?*

Stan is disappointed that his father isn't enjoying the mug, as Stan would love to have a beer mug just like it. When Stan bought the gift for his father, he did so without consulting Susan.

TEAM TOOLS

Giving a gift that you like can be easy to do. If the person receiving the gift has the same taste or preferences, it can work out well. However, consulting with your spouse will help you make a choice that's more likely to be valued and enjoyed by the recipient.

Stan: *"I've been thinking about a gift for dad."*
Susan: *"What did you have in mind?"*
Stan: *"Well I was thinking about one of those clear bottom beer mugs that I like."*
Susan: *(laughing) "Your dad doesn't drink beer!"*
Stan: *"Oh yeah, that's right."*
Susan: *(jokingly) "That's a great idea, you get your dad a mug, and he doesn't use it, and because you like your beer, he gives it to you!"*
Stan: *(laughing) "That's not a bad idea."*

Susan: *"Your Dad likes scotch, so why don't we get him some scotch glasses?"*

Stan: *"Great idea!"*

TIP: Before buying a gift, think about what that person really likes, rather than what you like.

Not the Bush, Not the Bush

Stan grew up in the city and loves to get out of town. He enjoys heading into the bush and camping. Susan also grew up in the city, but she likes it there. She finds going to the bush unpleasant, to say the least. Stan wants to buy some property about three hours from the city. The property is isolated and has no amenities. Susan likes creature comforts, and isn't in favour of the plan.

WHAT is happening here?

This couple is different in a number of ways, including how they like to spend their leisure time. A tug-of-war has begun between them. Susan not only likes the city, she enjoys reading and other hobbies, which she pursues in her home or neighbourhood.

TEAM TOOLS

Differences can be a hindrance to having a good time. Sometimes the differences are significant and the stretch to collaborate can be difficult. Even at these times, it's important to remember that what counts is "to love." If marriage is the priority, even big disparities can be bridged, and perhaps the reward will be larger than it would be if the collaboration was smaller.

Stan and Susan are enjoying each other's company more than ever since they reunited. They both want the other to manage the stresses of everyday life. Susan decides to reconsider the idea of buying the recreational property because she can see how relaxed Stan becomes when he's puttering around.

Stan is aware of Susan's preferences for amenities, and proposes that rather than camp, they find a little used trailer that could be hauled to the property for their accommodation. Susan agrees, and finds that she can pursue some of her hobbies like reading on the property. She is also learning more about nature from Stan, and he is discovering how relaxing reading can be, especially when it has to do with plant life!

TIP: Collaboration strengthens a marriage.

TINA AND TOM

Tina and Tom, like so many couples, are reactive listeners, but have been making efforts to reach out to one another more effectively. There are still the occasional ups and downs, but their relationship is generally in good shape.

Protect the Kids

Tom and Tina take their role as parents seriously. One of the ways they protect their children is by not exposing them to babysitters, for fear the children won't be safe. The result of this attitude is that Tina and Tom don't have much of a social life.

WHAT is happening here?

This cautious couple is staying home with their kids all the time. Because of their good intentions and fears, they aren't allowing themselves a break from their children, or their children a break from them.

TEAM TOOLS

Commitment to children as parents is expected and understood, but it can sometimes be overdone. It's important for kids to see their parents happy and strong as a couple. Before the children arrive, couples will usually date and spend time with friends, and this benefits them. It's possible to find reliable babysitters so that occasional dates can take place.

Children don't benefit from being overprotected, and there is evidence that such children can actually be more insecure than those who are allowed to experience life in a variety of safe ways.

Tom and Tina are very dedicated to their children and have come to realize that one of the ways they can love their kids is to have a strong marriage. They do their T-Times, and have been improving in their listening. They now enjoy going out for dinner or to a movie occasionally without the children.

At first, the kids put up a fuss because they weren't accustomed to their parents not being around. However, they adjusted to this new reality, and now wave goodbye when their parents go out. These outings are occasional but pleasurable for Tom and Tina.

TIP: **The kids will be fine if you go on a date by yourselves.**

VERONICA AND VINCE

This couple has been through a lot. They nearly broke up because of their poor communication and inability to consult with each other, but lately they've experienced many improvements.

Going Through the Motions

Veronica and Vince are out for dinner to celebrate Veronica's birthday. Veronica is excited to be out, and is chatting in an animated fashion, whereas Vince looks bored and isn't responding to Veronica's sharing.

WHAT *is happening here?*

This couple is on a date, which is a good thing. Actually, Veronica is on the date, and Vince is there physically, but not mentally. He isn't big on dinners out and is there as a kind gesture to Veronica for her birthday. He might as well have stayed home.

TEAM TOOLS

Going out on a date may be more one person's idea of a good time than the other's, but it can be a good way of getting a break from the routine of everyday life. It's important for the spouse who would rather stay home to enter into the outing with some enthusiasm so that it's enjoyable for his wife. On other occasions, she may agree to watch a hockey game with him, and can make the best of it as well.

Let's continue with the account of Vince and Veronica's date…

At a certain point, Veronica's enthusiasm touches Vince. He starts to respond to her and finds himself relaxing and enjoying himself in spite of not being that enthusiastic about dining out.

TIP: When we make an effort to enjoy what our spouse does, it can make a big difference to them. Share the interests of another person and make their day!

"Let's review the Tips…"

• Life is too important to be taken seriously!

• Dates or playtimes help to keep the fun in a marriage.

• Love your spouse the way he/she wants to be loved.

• Support is better than sarcasm.

• Laugh at your foibles.

• Talks and dates make a good combination.

• Be open to showing love in new ways.

• Praise in public is great; criticism is not!

• Be aware of your spouse's emotional needs.

• Love is creative.

• Before buying a gift, think about what that person really likes, rather than what you like.

- Collaboration strengthens a marriage.

- The kids will be fine if you go on a date by yourselves.

- When we make an effort to enjoy what our spouse does, it can make a big difference to them. Share the interests of another person and make their day!

CHAPTER TWELVE

Conclusion & Review

"Married for Life and Lovin' it"

It seems remarkable to me that I am finally writing a few words of conclusion for this book on marriage which is a reflection of the hours I have spent with couples who courageously maintained the hope that their marriage could ultimately fulfill their initial dreams of intimacy.

Certain themes have arisen again and again in counselling sessions and many of them have been charted in the preceding pages.

Why or how does a marriage succeed in this day and age? When a husband and wife make their marital relationship a priority and they are open to the change and the growth it brings. They make peace with the past and are unconditional in their love for each other.

In a successful marriage, both spouses make time for, and listen and speak with, each other on a feeling level. They struggle each day to improve their listening, not reacting to each other but truly hearing what each is saying.

Thriving marriages are made up of two very different people who perfect the art of consultation and collaboration. They know how to create joint plans and strategies. If the going gets rough they take a break using a Time-Out/Time-In technique.

Both spouses practice forgiveness and know how important it is to their ongoing wellbeing. They also laugh with each other and go on the occasional date on their own (without friends always around to distract them). They know how to express love to each other in ways that bring joy and peace.

If you have read this book and found it helpful or have any suggestions as to how it can be improved, please feel free to send me an email (info@denisboyd.com). Your ideas will be considered when the material is revised for further publication.

I will consider this book to be a success even if only one couple benefits from its content. This book is for couples who are willing to invest in their relationship and do whatever they can to improve it. Too many couples give up too easily and walk away from marriages that can be saved and rebuilt. Too many couples endure mediocre and boring unions.

I contend that it is possible to have a great marriage. There is no need to settle for less.

Denis's Definitions

Psychology is rampant with jargon, and many people don't understand these often confusing "code" words.

When working with couples, it has been my experience that the less jargon used, the better, and yet some unique terms and phrases seem appropriate and helpful to define ideas or strategies used in our counselling sessions.

I have found that a certain word or two can crystallize a concept. When offering couples strategies they can use to repair or improve their marriages, I find myself using terms that both catch their attention and capture the essence of a lesson. Some of the following definitions won't be found anywhere else, and represent a personal attempt to capture an idea. For this reason, I have described them as "Denis's Definitions."

The pronouns "he" and "she" are interchangeable as has been the case throughout the book.

APPEASER – A spouse who bends over backwards to avoid conflict with his partner. This person will rarely speak about topics that may upset his spouse, and tends to withhold his own opinion. He may eventually, however, blow-up over a seemingly small matter.

BALANCE – A healthy situation wherein a couple has numerous differences and a few similarities. The similarities are often threefold: values or philosophy of life, strength of character or "stubbornness," and insecurity or "woundedness."

BIRD DOGGER – A person who is upset and wants to wrap up an issue rather than leave it be, out of fear that it will "never get resolved." She will actually pursue a "withdrawing" spouse in hopes of keeping a debate going.

BLAMER – A person who blames others for his upset. This person reacts to the words or behaviours of others rather than listening for underlying feelings or thoughts. There is a lack of awareness of options for dealing with undesirable situations. This person tends to avoid taking responsibility for his role in an altercation.

BLAME GAME – When spouses focus on the faults or mistakes of the other and ignore their own role in a conflict. Some of the points made may have validity, but they aren't heard, as both partners, likely because of anger or hurt, are busy blaming the other for everything wrong between them.

BLIND SPOTS – Something we all have. There are aspects of ourselves we are unable to see or hear objectively. Marriage is a natural antidote to this dilemma in that spouses are usually able to see where the other is "blind," and are able to help each other in the challenges of everyday life.

BUILD 'N BLOW – A situation where a person stockpiles stress over time and periodically erupts when the proverbial "straw breaks the camel's back." This individual often describes himself as "easy-going."

CAVING IN – An instance where a person will express an opinion and then "fold" and go the way the other spouse wants to go. Often this individual is an appeaser or pleaser who dislikes conflict or hurting the feelings of others.

COLLABORATION – When two spouses acknowledge their differences on an issue and proceed to reach a joint solution. Each person goes from "my way" to "our way."

COMMITMENT PHOBIC – A person who is afraid to commit, and yet doesn't like to be alone. This person appears to want to be in a relationship and will promise whatever she thinks the other wants, but often doesn't follow through. She is usually deeply fearful of being controlled or hurt, or perhaps both. This is a situation wherein someone is afraid to be alone, and yet when with a significant other is also afraid to become emotionally intimate.

CONDITIONAL LOVE – A popular form of love whereby a spouse loves the other as long as she is being loved in return. Often there is a tendency to "keep score." Also known as "humanistic altruism."

COMPATIBILITY – Spouses who are very different from each other, but collaboratively work towards common goals.

DEAD MARRIAGE – A relationship that has deteriorated to the point where moving ahead seems impossible. This situation can be triggered by a crisis (an affair, for example) and leaves the couple with only two choices: rebuild it or end it permanently.

DEBRIEFING – A process by which spouses in a troubled marriage can attempt to identify weaknesses in their relationship. This is a first step towards change, which could lead to a "Tune-up" or complete "Rebuild." This debriefing process is effective only if each spouse focuses upon his or her role in the troubled relationship.

DEFENSIVENESS – A behaviour that is driven by emotion. When a person appears to be defensive, she may be feeling attacked, hurt, embarrassed, or other negative emotions.

DIVORCE (HIGH CONFLICT) – A breaking apart of a marriage because of violence, addiction, or mental illness. Often this sort of break-down is very difficult to repair.

DIVORCE (LOW CONFLICT) - A breaking apart of a marriage as the result of numerous small conflicts. This sort of breakdown is usually repairable, but one or the other spouse has given up without making an all-out attempt to make changes.

DOING BUSINESS – This is the last part of the T-Time (Talk-Time) where a couple explores their opinions, and where possible, moves towards a collaborative solution.

EMOTIONAL IMMATURITY – A condition whereby a person is an adult physically, but is emotionally still a child or a pre-teen. This situation can arise when an individual has had a traumatic experience as a child and hasn't been helped to work it through. It is as if the person is in arrested emotional development.

EMOTIONAL MATURITY – Refers to a person whose emotional growth has kept pace with her chronological growth. This individual is often empathic, motivated, disciplined, social and goal-oriented.

EYE CONTACT – Looking into the eyes of the other, at least some of the time, when conversing.

FLAT MARRIAGE SYNDROME – When a spouse says he loves his mate, but doesn't feel in love with her. This situation usually builds slowly over time, and is related to withholding frustrations or annoyances out of fear of hurting or annoying the other person (i.e. a "Fearful Talker").

GIVE AND GO – Each spouse is willing to negotiate differences of opinion with the aim of reaching a collaborative position.

GREAT MARRIAGE – A marital relationship where the spouses place their marriage at the top of their individual priority lists. This is not just a theoretical placement, but a lived reality on a daily basis. This couple has a deep and growing love for each other, and the word "boredom" is not in their vocabulary.

GROWING APART – A process whereby a couple places their personal growth and life activities ahead of the marriage.

GROWING TOGETHER – A process that happens when a couple places their marriage at the top of their priority lists. There is personal growth and adventure as well, but it isn't achieved at the expense of the marriage. Time is found regularly to touch base as a couple and to share in the experiences of the other.

INCOMPATABILITY – A condition that is the result of spouses not achieving collaboration. Their natural differences begin to be seen as irritations rather than assets.

INFORMATION SHARING – Conversation that is sometimes shared "on-the-run" about the details of everyday life, with minimal emphasis on the emotional state of the speaker or the listener.

INTIMACY – The result of a couple making each other a priority by having regular T-Times. When there are differences, which often there are, there is a willingness to collaborate.

JOINT PLAN – Created by a couple willing to blend their ideas. Often the result of Team Parenting.

LISTENING – Tuning into the emotions and ideas of the speaker, and giving feedback as to what is being heard.

LITTLE BOY/GIRL THINKER – An adult person who still thinks like a child. We learn to interact when we are children, and sometimes we enter adulthood still thinking and acting like the child we once were. This person may be emotionally immature or insecure due to unresolved historical issues.

MARRIED SINGLE – A person who is married, but is still thinking and acting like a single person.

MARITAL GOLDEN RULE – Loving one's spouse in a way that she wants to be loved. The Marital Golden Rule requires that each spouse consult with the other as to **how that person wants to be loved**, rather than **assuming** how to do it. It tends to be human nature to love the other person the way we like to be loved. However, because the other spouse is different, this may not be effective.

MARTYR – An appeaser or pleaser who is fearful of conflict or hurting his spouse. This person is often fearful that she will be abandoned or attacked if she lets thoughts or feelings surface, or if she challenges the other in any way. Often this person has underlying security issues.

MORNING PERSON – A person who is able to have an in-depth conversation only moments after awakening in the morning. This person will begin to fade around mid-evening, however, and is often or frequently married to a "Night Person."

MY WAY – When a person wants his way on an issue, and doesn't seem to care about the opinions or ideas of his spouse.

MUTUAL LOVE – Two spouses who love each other unconditionally.

NIGHT PERSON – A person who is able to have an in-depth conversation on almost any topic late in the day. This person doesn't know who he is until after mid-morning and a cup of coffee, and is often or frequently married to a "Morning Person."

OUR WAY – When spouses acknowledge each other's perspectives and collaborate on a solution.

PATTERNS – Established formats for communication used by a couple. Often these patterns don't work that well and lead to repetitive conversations about the same issues.

POWER STRUGGLE – What happens when spouses decide they are going to try and force the other to see or do things "my way."

PRIORITY ONE – What the marriage has to be to the spouses in order for it to be a great Marriage.

PRUNING – Spouses offering constructive criticism to each other with the aim of helping each other to become better people. If given harshly or dramatically, it can backfire, and a "Power Struggle" can result.

REACTIONARY LISTENER (Type 1) – One who is overwhelmed by his own feelings instead of hearing or tuning into the feelings of the other. This listener tends to ignore the feelings of the other, but will complain that his spouse isn't listening to him.

REACTIONARY LISTENER (Type 2) – One who is extremely focused on the feelings of the other, and ignores her own response. This listener will focus on trying to get rid of the other's mood by pleasing or appeasing. This listener takes responsibility for the feelings of the speaker.

REBEL – A spouse who in the past has kept peace "at all costs," but is no longer willing to do so. He now expresses his views assertively, sometimes even aggressively. The pendulum has swung to the other extreme. This person has a low tolerance for the feelings of the other spouse. In the past, he would take responsibility for his wife's feelings and try to appease them. Now he gets annoyed whenever his spouse is emotional.

REBUILD – A marriage that could have become a "low-conflict divorce" if something hadn't been done to repair it. This relationship has been reconstructed with improved patterns of interaction and a reawakened intimacy. The result is a marriage which is stronger than it has ever been.

SABOTAGE – A gesture made in an attempt to distance oneself from another person. This situation can arise during the reconstruction of a marriage by a spouse who is afraid of becoming too close, in case he gets hurt again.

SEXUAL INTIMACY – A situation that can occur when both spouses are feeling emotionally connected to each other. Often one spouse wants to have sex to connect emotionally, and the other wants to connect emotionally to have sex. Either spouse can play each role.

SLIPPAGE – A worry held by many rebuilding couples that old patterns of poor communication and collaboration will return. Such a worry is an indication of fear that changes won't be permanent. It eases over time, and eventually disappears.

T-TIME (Talk-Time or Tea-Time) CONVERSATION – A regular conversation in which there is an exchange of information or ideas and the feelings associated with them.

TEAM PARENTING – An approach to parenting that involves the parents sharing their ideas and strategies for parenting their children. Often there will be differences of opinion; however, this is an indication of "balance" in the relationship. The spouses accept their differences and collaborate on a "Joint Plan."

THINKING OUT LOUD – A process that can happen during a T-Time. For a talk to be meaningful, it isn't necessary to think for a long time and then speak about a conclusion. The thinking itself can be shared.

TIME-OUT – A technique to prevent useless arguing or fighting. For this to work well, both spouses need to agree in advance to use this strategy. It is wise to call it early on in the disagreement rather than waiting until a full blown argument is underway.

TIME-IN – The other half of the Time-Out strategy. After both spouses cool down and give some thought to their responsibility in the argument/fight, one spouse invites the other to resume the conversation. Each spouse begins by speaking about how he or she personally contributed to the previous altercation.

TONE – The edge or attitude in a person's voice that is almost always driven by emotion. In other words, a person who appears to be using a tone is perhaps upset or tired.

TRIAL SEPARATION – A step taken to revitalize a marital relationship. This step is often entered into with trepidation because of the worry that it might be permanent.

(Type 1) – A separation that occurs because one or both spouses are very distressed, and as a result, are finding it hard to make repairs. They know they need to work on their relationship, but have trouble dealing with built-up tension. They will live apart for a time, giving each other space while beginning to work on the "Rebuild."

(Type 2) – A separation that occurs because one person is convinced the marriage is in trouble and the other spouse is in denial. This separation can act as a wake-up call for the spouse in denial, who is often good at blaming his spouse for all the problems in the marriage.

TUNE-UP – Revitalizing a good marriage to make it even stronger.

UNCONDITIONAL LOVE – Giving without counting the cost, while challenging the other to love in return. The goal here is to have a mutual exchange of love. Parental love is usually unconditional, and spouses can love each other in the same way.

WALK 'N TALK – A T-Time (Talk-Time) conducted while walking together. Sometimes walking side by side can decrease the intensity of a conversation, and this makes it easier for reserved spouses to open up.

WITHDRAWER – A person who is upset or possibly threatened by a conversation and will shut down and pull back in self-defense. This gesture can be misinterpreted by a more outgoing and assertive person (Bird Dogger) as abandonment or rejection.

WORK THE MIDDLE – When a couple acknowledges their different perspectives on a given idea and then consciously moves towards a collaborative solution. They determine a plan that represents "Our Way."

Top Tips

Attitude

- It is OK to ask your spouse to change.
- Be honest about expectations from the get-go.
- Adjust to one another and for one another.
- Don't expect your spouse to be a mind reader.
- Marriage calls forth our potential.
- Your spouse can help you grow in confidence.
- Love by honouring the preferences of your spouse.
- Standing firm can help others confront issues from the past.
- The relationship counts, not the activity.
- Stretch into the world of the other and enhance intimacy.
- Finding time alone strengthens the bond.
- Strengthen your love by collaborating.
- Spend time together listening and talking.

Make Peace With The Past

- Discussing memories and the feelings that go with them can be liberating.
- Issues from the past can colour the present.
- Try to recall your past objectively.
- It is possible to resolve differences constructively.
- Share your full range of emotions.
- Cutting off contact doesn't resolve old hurts.
- Make peace with the past and live a happier life in the present.

• Sharing sad feelings is painful but healthy.

• Creative problem solving is better than abandonment.

• History need not repeat itself.

Unconditional Love

• Give freely.

• Listen without giving away your power.

• Your frame of reference can be a trap.

• Blaming blinds a person to his own faults.

• Unconditional lovers do not keep score.

• Kindness begets kindness.

• Love with your willpower.

• Love challenges us to be the best we can be.

T-Time (Daily Talk-Time or Tea-Time)

• Give structure to your talks.

• T-Times can be more enlightening than we anticipate.

• Check out each other's moods before doing "business."

• Awkwardness or feelings of artificiality will pass.

• Just act naturally.

• Thinking out loud works.

• Focus on feelings.

• Guess your spouse's feelings.

• T-Times can be surprising.

• What your day did to YOU, in terms of feelings, is the focus!!

• Unshared feelings can accumulate.

• Try walking for a low-key T-Time.

To Listen Is To Love

- Accept the feelings of another person.

- Acceptance leads to greater openness.

- Checking out feelings first makes for better listening.

- Listening but not commenting is appropriate at times.

- Hear the feelings behind the words.

- Changing the subject may indicate underlying discomfort.

- Listen first, clarify second and then listen some more.

- Checking out a tone of voice is better than reacting to it.

- Good listening leads to good listening.

- Holding on to issues can create a build'n'blow situation.

- When a feeling shows up in a conversation, it should become the focus.

- Listen always, even when talking.

- Judging can get in the way of good listening.

- Acknowledge feelings frequently.

- Personal feelings can take over and get in the way of hearing the other person.

- Feedback helps a speaker feel heard.

- Listening takes courage.

- Reactionary listening often begets reactionary listening.

- Help your spouse to communicate by listening well.

- Listen with empathy.

- Unchecked assumptions lead to misunderstandings.

- Feelings are hiding behind defensiveness.

Consultation & Collaboration

- Share information with your spouse before sharing it with friends.
- Move from my way to our way.
- Collaborate to enrich your marriage.
- Consultation leads to joint plans.
- Watch for the impact of your words on the other person.
- Collaboration means to meet in the middle.
- When your spouse seems not to be listening, it may be that she is disagreeing.
- Differences make for balance in a relationship.
- Your spouse can see where you are blind.
- Are you looking for yourself in a spouse?

Time-Out/Time-In

- Calling a Time-out prevents a power struggle.
- Learning from our mistakes enriches a relationship.
- Call a Time-In when both of you are ready to do so.
- Self correction is the key to a good Time-In.
- Time-out/Time-in prevents recurring arguments.

Forgive Frequently

- Feel first and then forgive.
- Forgiveness doesn't make what happened acceptable.
- Fear can get in the way of forgiveness.
- It is OK to forgive and not forget.
- Old memories may still have feelings attached.
- Forgiveness helps to stop the Blame Game.

After The Crisis - The Rebuild

• Too much change, too fast, backfires!

• In the Rebuild (fog), move ahead carefully, one step at a time.

• A successful rebuilt marriage is stronger and healthier than the old relationship.

• Commit to trying to commit.

• Talking and good listening can be early stage lovemaking.

• Renewed sexual intimacy warms up gradually over time.

• Rebuilding trust takes time.

Laugh, Play & Encourage

• Life is too important to be taken seriously!

• Dates or playtimes help to keep the fun in a marriage.

• Love your spouse the way he/she wants to be loved.

• Support is better than sarcasm.

• Laugh at your foibles.

• Talks and dates make a good combination.

• Be open to showing love in new ways.

• Praise in public is great; criticism is not!

• Be aware of your spouse's emotional needs.

• Love is creative.

• Before buying a gift, think about what that person really likes, rather than what you like.

• Collaboration strengthens a marriage.

• The kids will be fine if you go on a date by yourselves.

• When we make an effort to enjoy what our spouse does, it can make a big difference to them. Share the interests of another person and make their day!